M000083335

Jericho's Journey:

A Journey of Self Discovery through Progression

By Samuel Martinez IV

Copyright © 2019 Samuel J. Martinez IV

@smartineziv

All rights reserved. No portions of this book may be used or reformatted in any way via electronic, mechanical, photocopying, scanning, or otherwise without the written permission, except in the case of brief quotations embodied in critical articles and reviews.

Disclaimer: Due to the fact that the internet moves at such a rapid rate, it is possible that some of the references in this book may be subject to change or become invalid. The views in this book are solely those of the author.

The author does not profess as an expert in any of the fields also included in the book. In addition does advise you speak with medical professionals before embarking on any changes to physical routine such as diet and exercise. The intentions are to only inform and educate on different perspectives as to help you discover who you are within this cycle of fulfillment.

Printed in the United States of America

ISBN: 9781075494390

Contents

Dedication

For my family; my kids, Jeremy and Raelynn as well as my wife, Kaitlyn. Without your faith in me I could have never put this all together.

Preface

This is not a self-help book. This is a book on self-awareness. This book isn't going to solve all of your problems but rather serves as another perspective to reference. I am nobody special. I am an average husband, father, writer, podcaster, and now an author. I have never had extravagant material possessions. To be quite honest I've barely managed to get this far. I'm not even sure how? Between countless bills, a mountain of debt, expectations up to the wazoo! I have to be in multiple places at once putting out multiple fires at once. I remember when I was a kid, I always felt like I had to take care of and be secure for everyone else. I went above and beyond with this crazy hope that things would eventually get better. Nope. Not even close. Things got much harder. I cannot change you. We cannot change anyone. What we can do, however, instead is become an example from within ourselves so that we can set the standard for others. This book will definitely help with that.

If you've opened this book and are reading this page then surely you are feeling specific ways about life right now. Whether it's not being where you thought you would be by now or maybe the job wasn't what it seemed? You don't have the money you want, or perhaps you simply just lack the drive and motivation even to find what it is about life that gives it meaning at all? No matter what you feel, these emotions are both essential and healthy. So take them in, all of them.

Feel them, and rejoice in the fact that we actually have the capability of being aware of these emotions whether they are positive or not. Seeing as though we are inherently emotionally driven creatures, and virtually the only species that can think abstractly, it is always important to at the very least be grateful of our emotions and let them know that they are being heard. So take in everything and feel it. We will get into more about feelings in part four, but for now, it is essential to know that these are a part of you and make up a good portion of what shapes our self-belief. So always take into account that they can be both reflections and driving forces for the necessary action you've either made or have yet to take to further yourself.

Now to fully understand what this book will be about, you must first understand where this knowledge is coming from. There have been disappointments, losses, deaths, and mistakes that have pushed me so far back that I kid you not, I literally thought sometimes that time travel could, in fact, be possible. The more mistakes that were made, the more frequently I would find myself dwelling on the past as if my mind were the DeLorean from back to the future and went 88 miles per hour back in time (if you're a millennial, Google it). This life, although filled with its ups and downs, has given me blessings that I could not even begin to repay, let alone describe. It's crucial to break completely free from the mistakes you've made when beginning your journey because getting lost in that endless loop can alter your perception of what you believe can even become possible, and belief is where it all starts. If you cannot also believe in yourself, how is anybody else supposed to?

I want to live with no regrets, and I encourage others to do the same. I have a passion for helping people find their version of success through progression and awareness. I want to share my personal growth, and how you can also take opportunities to become better each day and capitalize on the opportunities, you may not have been able to notice otherwise. You need to be observant and pay attention to those coincidences or those times where things just felt right.

What I'm going to share throughout this book is what I believe to be a kind of Rolodex system that has helped me go from situations of constant helplessness and depression to days of fulfillment and progression! With the occasional stressors of course but the key takeaway is that your current location does not have to be the only situation. It's you that decides where your mind goes, and it's ultimately you that determines how far you desire to go. When you create a sanctuary in the brain, it starts to become quieter, allowing you to organize thoughts and optimize your levels of reach in that potential exponentially!

As a father and a husband, it is scary to know whether or not you are making the right decisions. I have made so many mistakes without anyone to help guide or mentor me. I was taught instead to believe that values were most important and that hard work would give you money.

Then you'd live happily ever after.

Nobody ever told me about the repercussions of having an average mindset where the rat race is the law of the land. Upon realizing everything through my own faults eventually ending me up into near homelessness and without a family, I have since taken things as challenges and with it am now able always to do more than most with ambition and optimism. Also being very depressed and unfulfilled, the worst combination is a crazy hard work ethic with no focus or purpose. I continue to be competitive and never back down. Life has taken me on a journey, but it's made me into who I am today. My life has not been the easiest, but at the same time, I'm aware that not a single person in this world's life has or ever will be.

It is both naive and ignorant to assume anyone has a comfortable life no matter how well they seem to have it together. People have their problems, money, or no money, but seeing the difference and the denominations of those problems when broken down can become how the solutions are created. The foundations of life are where these solutions are discovered. They stem from a strong, sturdy, and grounded foundational mindset that won't allow movement or sway you back and forth with opinions like the wind shifts a sailboat in the water.

For too long, I had let so much cloud my judgment that I used self-sabotage as an outlet and began to honestly believe that I had little worth because everything was happening to me. Poor baby, right? This was my thought process, though. I would blame the entire world, leaving me with no control and allowing my emotions to just completely take over and drive my focus as well as my decisions. Which in turn allowed so much self-doubt that I actually did believe my worth had depleted. This can cause anyone to resort to self-sabotage; how many of us know someone that indulges in excessive drinking, smoking, shopping, etc.?

In essence, that is where this book comes in. The goal for this is to provide a guidebook or 'alleyway' for you to reference whenever you may be feeling certain emotions and to one, know that you are not alone; and two, have that kind of Rolodex to go through and pinpoint what is going on and how to attack the problems in your life. All the while showing that an average person can have an above average mindset, and in turn, be happy even with the bare minimum. It isn't enough in the year of 2019 to just simply work hard and have that be the end all be all, nor can it just be wished upon much as a star or birthday, it honestly does not work like that.

In conclusion, there is much that was both taught and uncovered by me. I do not attest to being a professional nor a 'self-help' coach, but these instead are all of the things that have helped me lead an abundant life and be able to even talk with people on a level playing field regardless of income or wealth. The wealth lies inside of you, and it is untapped potential power. It isn't about the money, and the sooner you realize this, the sooner you will revel in the fact that it comes in as soon as you do not make it the primary form of accomplishment and success. That's neither here nor there but without further ado, let's get into this book and begin to shape life for the better.

Let's Be Realistic

"I think everybody should get rich and famous and do everything they ever dreamed of so they can see that it's not the answer."
-Jim Carrey

This book is not a get rich quick guide to AdSense or a million followers or even money in general. This book is instead intended to be an informative way to put things into perspective whenever you start to feel your harmony is off the balance in life between your fulfillment and your hopelessness. Most believe that the rich get rich because they get lucky, some already know that isn't the truth. Luck happens when preparation meets opportunity. Meaning when you're ready, good things will come.

The problem with this is not the statement itself, but rather that people are lazy and feel entitled. Most people feel as though they listen to one interview and are all of a sudden experts and are ready to take on the world in that field. Without ever genuinely experiencing the information that they are even providing. Realistically, it is about finding out who you are. Not the version of you that you feel everyone else wants you to be, but the, you, that you want to be. Whether it be through experimentation or just by gaining new knowledge to apply in every day. By doing this, you are also developing a perspective as to what you are naturally good at versus what you just love to do because they may not be the same. Look at all of the celebrities that have other passions they never knew about, such as Jim Carrey and his painted artwork (which is beautiful by the way I recommend you go check it out).

This is where it all begins. Write a list of every single thing you love or love to do. If you're not sure what that is, then stop reading this book and figure that out before you continue. You've got to find a passion in life because that ultimately leads to progression into your purpose! So what do you love? Riding bikes, scuba diving, journaling, watching YouTube? Whatever it is, begin to dedicate more time around those things. Involve one by one for at least an hour a day. If its tennis, buy a racquet one weekend and go play, it doesn't matter. This though is how you start to form that passion and find what you are really interested and get lost in. Have fun with this new found experimentation.
Once you've pinpointed this, you can now create the life around it outside of what you do currently. Keep this in mind, there is a famous guy named 'Ninja' that was on the cover of ESPN magazine for the video game Fortnite. If that very statement doesn't put things into perspective, nothing will. It is an entirely different time now, and most people just haven't been exposed to the right thoughts, ideas, and people that will allow for the vision in realizing how to obtain it. Well, after reading this book, not only will you have a clear vision, but you will also have the drive, ambition, and self-belief to attack everything with intensity and focus.

In the first part, you will learn about my fulfillment cycle, and when you read about it, begin to revolve the 'not making excuses' concept around the baseline principles for your betterment. It will also make it easier to see what kind of decisions will be in your best interest or if they are just based on the merit of you simply 'wanting' outcomes.

Everything I've learned, everything I've done has all been done by in the meantime. The books, the videos, the podcasts, the interviews, the research, the experiments, the applications of all of my learnings, my writings, everything has all been done underneath the helping and giving of others. The reason most parents won't do things because they have kids, in my opinion, is because they fail to understand how to block the level of time that is required to be taken. To prevent this time out correctly, you need to use what I call, The Power of Meantime.

So how did I write this book? Well, the answer is simple… The meantime. I had no time between the Podcast I started (please tune in), the videos I was trying to figure out how to make, working out five days a week, figuring out how to come into the social media world, and how to navigate the ways in which I wanted to do everything, taking care of both of my kids. Did I mention helping build my brother in laws home improvement business at this time? This alone involved ten hour days painting an entire house by myself with carpet cleanings as well as concrete and trash pickup jobs when it slowed down. For me to do all of that, it didn't even seem plausible, let alone practical to write a book.

However, even after all of that, my adjustment to write this book while still managing adequate amounts of rest was to begin at three o'clock every morning. Yup. I literally got up every morning at three o'clock just to write this very book. I have always been an early bird, and I figured this was the quietest time even to make an attempt and boy, was I right! I have been able to get more of my writings done in the morning than I ever thought possible. To top it off, it is in the morning when I feel most alive and creative. My point is that sometimes first, to get to that next level, you are going to need to really, truly realize that it is going to have to be in the meantime. There are no lulls, there is no free time, there is only meantime.

Meantime for me has always just meant the wasted time that I have for myself, which is all of the free time I used to feel I had. I used to be the first one to complain about not having time. That's when it hit me that instead of complaining about it, I need to become smarter about it. Any hours I have not explicitly set aside for my family, are times when I am either posting (follow me on all social media), writing, learning, reading, planning, creating, working, or trying to build an organization in the midst of it all to help aid others that are struggling with that guide to fulfillment. So when do I rest? Well, I get about six or seven hours and go to bed around eight or nine o'clock at night. I also try and get a nap in during the day, but that doesn't happen too often.

The Power of Meantime is a different perspective. Much like setting aside money to invest. You set aside little increments, and it compounds over time. The same happens with how you grow. Make sure the so-called "free" time isn't "down" time because it's not actually free. It is costing time, and we only get 86,400 seconds in a day. So how much of that is being invested into your "mean" time or your "progression" time. When you make progress, you get better. When you get better, you level up.

Think of videos games. Much as you battle to defeat different levels, you move forward, and the game gets harder. This is what happens in life, but just as the video games allow, experience also ensures you have the tools necessary to solve the challenge. The universe gives you what you ask for and so if you're sights are not set you will become distracted. This is why most people don't get past a few episodes on their platforms or why they never follow through. Instead of accepting the challenge we set it aside assuming it will come to us later so now we feel blocked, and we control the things we think are easy like watching videos or Netflix or drinking excessively or stop doing other productive stuff because we feel discouraged that we cannot get through this damn level.

This is when you need to take advantage. Don't take the Power of Meantime for granted because sooner or later your mind will be consumed by the demands of people around you so much that you begin to conform instead of break free. Most people struggle because they feel as though it isn't going to happen. However, it's not that end that should keep you going, it's the hope itself that you need to revel in. So many people want the happiness they want the money they want the fulfillment, but they fail to see that it takes patience, persistence, and complete hard work. They know the result and the payoff and not the struggle, not the rejection, not the doubt, not the disbelief they may encounter. I'm here to tell you it takes work, it takes courage, it takes humility, it takes tolls on you and your thoughts, your judgment, and your beliefs also. If you pursue your way through it however what I can promise is that regardless of the level of life you desire, just by beginning here at "meantime" you will start to grow beyond that of the people around you and be the change instead of waiting for it to come to you.

Now that we've covered meantime get started. Get going, the next time you're bored or are doing something that is allowing you to desire more than you should be doing more. It isn't enough to wish. Our dreams only go as far as we do. So if we go beyond our limits, then the universe will provide you with just that. Ideas beyond borders. So go and start to learn everything you love to learn about and become who you always wanted to be. It's going to be hard, but the harder and more intelligently you're able to work earlier on it will triple that investment later when it truly matters.

My Intent

I intend to help be the inspiration to people that I never had. I had to take the initiative to learn every day, and in doing so have become healthy, confident, fulfilled, and a productive person majority of the time, and isn't that the goal? What I realized was that it wasn't about money at all. I had to choose to take an opportunity to quit my job to help build a business. I had to decide to dictate my own life by developing a framework, and I want others to have the same ability. It isn't enough to simply work hard. Life is more complicated than that, and I hope with all that I have experienced and in the way that this book is written you too can find this sense of guidance within yourself and can grow substantially through progression and belief. Now that you know my story and intent let's truly begin the journey of self-discovery.

Start Your Foundation

Much as a tree has roots, basically our internal body is our roots, and our external body is our tree. Everything begins from inside the body, starting with the brain, stemming into the food you consume and how that food is processed. We need first to be aware of what goes into our bodies, to begin to be healthy and be able to have any type of control over the face of adversity. In knowing this, it is crucial to make sure diet, exercise, as well as stretching, moving around and being outside, are continuously and consistently playing a role in your daily habits. There are cells throughout our body that are continually changing and evolving. Although I may not know all of the science behind it, the basis of what is happening inside the body should at least be identified. The food we eat contains what we need, and this allows us to feel good or bad, happy, or sad. The things most people do not know, is what is in that food that is eaten is mostly containing processed sugar and flour which spike insulin levels and have been known to cause, in excess amounts, diabetes as well as several other health complications. This is why it is essential to be aware and begin to form the foundation of which the desired outcome can be achieved. Set yourself up for success.

Most actors that need to gain and lose weight for movie roles also need to work out as well as eat with stringent guidelines. Actors such as Mark Wahlberg agree that between diet and exercise, what is preferred are the workouts. However, the eating right, having mindfulness, and controlling the emotions are all that entails the health pillar of fulfillment. In the next chapter, the cycle of fulfillment will be talked about, and it will go over building health, relationships, and the steps to find your purpose and how to apply it into daily life.

No matter what your idea of success is, it will always be able to be achieved, but that's not what it is ultimately about. It's about who you're becoming. I believe most people want money until they realize what they actually desire. As they go through their emotions and begin to sift between themselves asking the more profound questions, and reconfiguring the stories in which have been narrated within their heads. It will also discuss how to be grateful and how to focus energy on things that matter and not just things that are attributing to the excess stress.

Stress itself can be a terrible catalyst to many diseases, so it is vital to our health to manage it. It can be caused by several factors such as a job, co-worker, spouse, environment, finances, school, the list goes on. Other chapters of this book will help isolate and identify the underlying causes and begin to let go of the unwanted stress. As you can clearly see, I am nobody special. I am an average husband, father, writer, podcaster, and now an author. I just figured out how to tap into something that would allow me to feel fulfillment from within and be able to have faith that things are happening as they are supposed to. Hope is for the past, faith is for the future, and we are the path. Now, let's get into the cycle and how it operates in our daily life!

Cycles & Villains

Prologue

Jericho never had much of anything. He was the type of person that was always taught to make due. "Be resourceful!" his parents would say. They worked a typical nine to five and would often be left at home to get his brother and sister ready for school in the mornings. He even stayed home with them on the weekends. What would they eat that day? Majority of the time that would be the question he would ask come three o'clock every afternoon. With his mother and father out working late, the kids really never received much benefit other than values they were now being forced to become accustomed to. This really created a lot of doubt whether or not he or his family would ever receive any goodness in this life. His worth began to fall, and he wasn't exposed to very much positivity. He was not in the best environment, a mobile home, in a downtown trailer park on the "not-so-good" part of town.

His childhood wasn't spectacular, actually quite the opposite. Which led him to the conclusion that good people are simply meant to suffer and have less. While others are expected to receive abundance regardless of merit or character, at least as though it appeared. It never seemed fair, but it seemed the way of the world. He would get angry from time to time and extremely frustrated. The stream of thoughts kept consistently perpetuating more doubt, more anxiety, and more fear. His friends would pass by with their families on his way home from school, and through their gaze, he could feel their false sense of confusion and prejudice.

From the day he was born, his family never even had a car. He and his siblings would always have to walk everywhere together, and his parents did the same. He was still running to catch the bus to get to school because he was busy helping manage the house as well as reading and doing school work and getting everyone ready. He was always questioning his existence. He was grateful to have the breath in his lungs, but he was confused as to why him? Why his family? Even more, he wondered how he could get the things that he saw others taking advantage of. He often started to question what he could do differently. He was lost but hopeful. He was impatient yet curious. He was not the most capable nor the most organized, but the one advantage he knew he had was his promise always to try his absolute best to change things one day.

Throughout his teen life, he would still find himself desiring the things that others had, and always told himself if he ever got anything close to that he would be absolutely grateful to have gained that level of

achievement. His parents were never around, and he was the oldest, so to get that type of acknowledgment was not very common at all. Plus he never said anything about his financial or living situations at home. He never wanted to burden others with his issues, so he kept to himself and instead always tried to learn something new so that one day there would be no more suffering. Still though, as he kept growing up, the cycle continued. It even got to a point where he could not get any help with school work because not even his parents understood it nor had the time.

He knew it was because they were trying to secure their own fears, but it was definitely hard, to say the least, to never have the ones you admire most never truly take the moments to focus on being present instead of material objects. The only reason he was able to really come to grips and be empathetic of it all was that he always recalled the night of not having the lights on or the water running. Or even running at a warm temperature at that! There were plenty of times he'd come home to all three being shut off and would just sit in the silence, cold and hungry until mom and dad could get back to shed some of their own light on the situation.

Seeing all of this made him never really sure of what to actually believe works. He started to notice at this point that some people were not putting forth much valuable effort yet were way better off than his family and became distraught pondering the fact that he could not figure this out. So he just kept exploring and doing what he thought might be best, but little did he know how distracted he was also becoming.

Post-graduation, he never really had close friends.

He wasn't a negative person to want to be around, he was just a little socially awkward. Some would look at him and think he was crazy or trying to act better than everyone, but he still had a feeling there was more to life. He began to notice the ways other people would spend their time. They would binge-watch the latest Netflix shows and eat out of boredom. He would occasionally partake and laugh a bit at some of the more humorous programs, but he always felt like he could be doing more. He noticed many different forms of productivity, and that was what instilled that promise to himself that he would always keep his focus on getting himself out of his situation and helping his family. He would look up at the stars and just have this unwavering faith come through him that everything was going to be alright with hard work and that's what gave him strength every day. He knew there had to be more, and that all of the suffering, hard work, and poise he had shown thus far would not be all for nothing.

On a beautiful snowy, winter morning, he received a bike from a family member during the holidays as a Christmas present, and that was one moment he had never forgotten. Every day had been the same, just one continuous cycle, but everything changed once he got the bike. As soon as he got it, he began riding down the trails in local terrain and leveled up fast to the advanced stages where he would compete and continuously be challenging his efforts. It was crazy how good he was able to become in such a short amount of time, and so he soon let that reflect into his everyday life. He started taking care of himself, and things were looking up! Finally, after all that time, he was in a place where he could say he was doing well and feeling alive. It was

after a couple of years that he decided to hang the bike up for a while and begin running. Taking him back to his roots of catching buses and getting to and from, but this time as an actual sport. He fell in love with it and found himself running multiple marathons every year at that point. Even becoming one of the top runners in the country! He was always getting better and better. He made himself, and more importantly, his family proud. He went from nothing to something. Most people have a hard time even going anywhere from nothing!

One night Jericho had a dream he was in a treacherous desert surrounded by lifeless wind, blistering heat, and a jagged knife-like pain piercing at his feet. His fear was rising. The vivid imagery was so abstract and real, it looked as though it was from another planet or from a new sci-fi movie! He wasn't scared of creatures or anything like that, he was instead afraid of what felt like imminent death. He felt dehydrated, frail, and weak. He looked up and saw the night skies bursting with stars, and could distinguish distant galaxies. He didn't know how he was able to keep moving forward. At the base of a nearby mountain, he noticed relics of ancient civilizations as the vast dryness continued to infiltrate throughout his entire body as well as visible from the terrains dead energy. He came to, enough to start pondering whether or not he was acting out an Alice In Wonderland scene when he glanced over at the snow-capped volcanoes to the left. Then suddenly, turns to the right and finds himself gazing in awe at the multicolored rainbow mineral deposits covering the valley. He regained focus, noticing something further down. A silhouette. As he got closer, he realized it was a person! Just as he was

about to scream for help, and perhaps a clue as to where he was, he tripped, fell onto the salty moon rocks and instantly awoke!

"Woah!" he gasped! Trying to recount what had just happened.

It’s A Circle

“Like a circle, it goes on forever. It's not like a triangle, triangle have corners. It's like a circle” - Rob Schneider, I Now Pronounce You Chuck and Larry.

Growing up, I always wondered what ‘the meaning of life’ was. Perhaps you’ve experienced this same curiosity, and that's why you opened the book in the first place? One thing I realize now though is that regardless of the number of stories I've heard or experiences I've had or even the knowledge I’ve acquired, I've come to the notion that it all has come down to one recurring theme.

There’s a middle ground to it. It's the reason people of status can become successful and why the person that came from nothing can receive that same form of success. Or why someone with little to nothing can remain so happy all the time as if nothing shakes them. I have broken these commonalities down into easily digestible principles that can always be referenced back to. First, let's begin with the concept of cycles.

The Water Cycle:

The cycle of processes by which water circulates between the earth's oceans, atmosphere, and land, involving precipitation as rain and snow, drainage in streams and rivers, and return to the atmosphere by evaporation and transpiration.

Photosynthesis:

The process by which green plants and some other organisms use sunlight to synthesize foods from carbon dioxide and water. Photosynthesis in plants generally involves the green pigment chlorophyll and generates oxygen as a byproduct.

The Life Cycle:

The series of changes in the life of an organism including reproduction.

The Four Seasons:

Winter, spring summer and fall.

These are just a few examples of different cycles that are a part of everyday life. There is also actual Recycling as well!

The process of converting waste materials into new materials and objects.

I'm sure we can reach a consensus that cycles are everywhere and they are constantly working in different ways within everyday life.

The Main Point:

Until I reached this full understanding that cycles

are what life consists of, that's when I was able to realize that everything comes down to pattern recognition. The patterns are what allow differentiation to the fact that nothing is permanent. Think about it? You can map out the next part of the cycle because it's always constant. It's what happens within that's decided whether it's beautiful or not. The constant of patterns themselves don't change, and the flow of cycles don't alter, but perspective within them can. When you realize that, you soon figure out that the power of contrast is what keeps us ready for the storms that arise and maintains our presence when the calm is upon us. Being able to know this off the cuff keeps you ahead of the curve.

The reason why it is so important to know this is because, much as Jericho has, the way that I've lived life has been very painfully dedicated to the faith that there has always been something better to come. I've never had the correct guidance, and so I lived through trial and error. Adversity has always been my mentor. After my breakthrough moment in life where I almost lost everything, I finally began to try and simplify what I could. Through the years, I stumbled upon a framework directly relating to cycles. The Fulfillment Cycle is something I believe in. I think it gives everyone the ability to create sustainable…

- **Gratitude For Today**
- **Momentum For Tomorrow**
- **Energy For The World**
- **Empathy For Others**
- **Awareness For Ourselves**

The main pillars in this cycle contain that of, Mental,

Physical and Spiritual Health, Relationships, and Purpose. I believe focusing on these, you can cycle through and receive what I call Baseline Principles.

- **Mental Health gives us gratitude.**
- **Physical Health gives us momentum.**
- **Spiritual Health gives us better energy.**
- **Relationships grant us empathy for others.**
- **Purpose grants us awareness within ourselves.**

So why these specifically? Let me explain,

My entire life has consisted of needing to "recycle" through all of these universal principles and they have turned me from being ungrateful, very lost and extremely manipulative to truly forgiving myself and being able to look in the mirror with the acceptance of the father and the husband that I know I can continue to be. In every moment of every day. Not only that but utilizing gratitude, momentum, energy, empathy, and awareness has solidified what I want to do and become for the future. It's taught me to be present and be happy regardless of outcome or income.

Life is about fulfillment within ourselves first, and that can only begin within each day. Slowly but surely using progression to get to where we need to go, we will not only take more action but also take note and audit what works versus what doesn't. So let's really get into the secrets of how to create a fulfilling and abundant life from the inside out. We will begin first and foremost with a breakdown of the purple clouds or villains that may be hovering over all of our heads and reigning fire down upon us.

Villains

"Just because you have superpowers, that doesn't mean your love life would be perfect. I don't think superpowers automatically means there won't be any personality problems, family problems or even money problems. I just tried to write characters who are human beings who also have superpowers." – Stan Lee

Who is your favorite villain? For some reason mine always reverted back to Venom, the villain in the Spiderman Comic books. For those unfamiliar, the character is a free forming parasite. It can latch onto a host and basically have the freedom to be able to do just about whatever it desired. In addition to that, being an outcast on Earth as an alien, maybe I even related to the fact that he was misunderstood a bit.

Nonetheless, my point is that life has the same types of villains. Ones that latch onto us as the host and continue to influence us to make poor decisions. Until it is done and then onto the next. The worst part of it all is that we may not even be aware that it has latched onto us!

Some of these are not just physical. Some are internal, mental, and spiritual. Either way, we all have our own form of them.

The only way to truly combat these villains of life is to incorporate what I call,

PRA:

- **Realize your superpower. (Potential)**
- **Unlock it with self-belief. (Reach)**
- **Fully surrender. (Aggression)**

Much as any comic book portrays, we are the path of our own hero's journey. We are the only ones with the powers to get rid of the dark clouds that hover over the village. People are counting on each of us in our own way, and this is going to be the time where all of the areas in life we have been scared to look will come to light. The truth of it all is that the villains stem from insecurities within the self so depending on the resistance level, and the depth of the darkness, that will depend on the persistence level of the opponent. Remember, the harder you fight, the smarter they get. The key is to outsmart them as you outwork them. So to figure out how to do that, let's get to know the most common forms of villains:

Fear Is Bliss

"On the other side of fear is absolute bliss". -Will Smith.

Will Smith is one of my all-time favorite people in the world. He is an extraordinary actor, rapper, and now YouTube vlogger that recently has been doing some pretty incredible things. His latest stunt was him skydiving over the Grand Canyon! The plane flew up, he jumped out, and it was one of the most beautiful things you had ever seen. Just a free fall and after they landed they asked him about the experience, and his message was apparent. Fear shouldn't stop you! Even if everyone thinks that you're crazy for trying something new and for doing what you always wanted to, it shouldn't matter what anyone else thinks. You matter, and it matters to you, so why shouldn't it actually matter? Fear stops most people because they feel like something terrible will happen. This is false.

If you eliminate fear from the equation or allow for a state of gratitude when making a decision, that's when you start to realize that regardless of the result, if you're able to be satisfied that you even made a decision, it unlocks more doorways for exploration. This can give you potential information inside you may need for your journey. Majority of the time, the things that cripple us from making any real change are fear, ego, and distraction. Fear, however, plays a significant factor in how we perceive things. This creates confusion towards fear and danger. That seeps through into our daily life. Our subconscious reaction is to refrain from the fear and not attack it head-on. When we make decisions from fear, we are being irrational and selfish in what we could potentially be giving ourselves, holding back instead of being who we know we can be.

Fear signals a fight or flight response. What people don't realize though is that the fight or flight response is designed in nature to continue our survival. So living based on fear, in essence, means you are surviving through life and not living it. Try making a decision not based on fear but rather, practicality. Ask yourself, "will this decision further the trajectory of where I want to be?" or ask yourself if it will hinder growth altogether. Of all of the success stories you read or hear about the one underlying tonality of what the basis was in which they all began their career is fear. It can be a power that can change your life, or it can be the very thing stopping you. That choice, however, is ultimately dictated by our daily actions and desire to keep the pursuit of your goals alive.

What's the first decision you make every morning?

- *Is it to go get coffee?*
- *Is it to stress the day that lies ahead?*
- *Or maybe it is to hit that snooze button?*

Either way, our thoughts and our days begin with our first decision of the day, and this should be for you to be courageous. For you to say out loud to yourself that you will be happy and not fearful of anything that may happen that day. This decision creates focus, and most people don't realize the power that it gives us. It immediately takes us from being fearful and nervous of our days into a transition of offense and willingness to take on any challenges.

This is something I had to learn head on. I was always brought up with being comfortable and working within the confines of where I was and not really pursuing action but reacting to what life would throw at me. You cannot, however, expect to play defense the whole game and win. You've got to take offense at least once to score. If you want to take some homework away from this, it is that you need to become courageous and try new things.

Start by telling yourself every morning that you're going to be happy and willing to take on any challenges that day, and I mean physically out loud! It sounds very cliché, but you will shift your mind to the offense for the day. Go into every work day as the battle, and let the meantime be your training. One day you will be a master, but it takes strength, resilience, and aggression to get there and to create that foundation takes grueling effort. The question people forget to ask though is if they're willing to suffer for what they believe is possible?

The Three E's – Ego

"The ego is only an illusion, a very influential one. Letting the ego-illusion become your identity can prevent you from knowing your true self. Ego, the false idea of believing that you are what you have or what you do, is a backward way of assessing and living life." -Wayne Dyer

If you take for example all of the most sustainably successful people out there in all genres; Warren Buffett, Tony Robbins, Jeff Bezos, Jim Carrey, Drake, Beyonce, Jay Z, LeBron James, Tom Brady, and even going as back as far as Genghis Khan, all of these people had and have one thing in common, and that is awareness of ego. Not overcompensating too excessively, nor undervaluing themselves too little. Seemingly exposing this middle ground. However, when you analyze the different parts of their lives in totality the commonality over how they were able to become aware of it was the fact that they became curious. They were all constantly learning as opposed to replaying the wrong cycle system.

The ego is one of the most deadly, yet empowering parts of the human mind because it can become inflamed at any moment without us even realizing it has happened. Having excessive amounts of ego can prevent us from seeing things clearly because we get caught up in the smaller version of ourselves. It can make us feel entitled to things, create blame, and excuses for why we don't do things, allowing for false realities to plague your dreams. It can be a double-edged sword because we can also have too little ego and lack the confidence ever to take a risk. Ego is like the immature kid sitting in the back seat, wanting to make decisions for you. Similar to emotion, the important thing is to recognize and acknowledge that the ego is there but not allow total strength or power. This is where logic and reason come in.

Have you ever noticed when you are arguing with a spouse or a loved one and once logic and reason come into it, all of a sudden the person gets mad that the reactive engagement isn't on the same wavelength as their emotional state? Or basically, they get angry because you didn't get upset. The ego gets upset when we refuse to pay attention to the part that wants that instant sort of gratification, but when we can control this and maintain a level of self-esteem that is both practical and reliable, this can set everything up in a much better way.

We have mirror neurons in our brain that actually try to mimic that of others, so this is why you see people laugh together or yawn. It is the same concept for the ego when it comes to arguments. If both people in the above discussion are thinking logically and have their egos in check, well then this typically allows for a great and meaningful conversation. Providing an excellent environment for communication and connection to grow and progress to become stronger with a much more robust foundation. The ego will resort to arguments because it thrives on competition and once that becomes stronger than our own need for competitiveness with ourselves, then we've already lost the battle.

So what do we do? Well, we become friends with our ego, because when you know you're ego, you can identify your ego, and when you can do that you can reference back with enough knowledge to keep the ego in its place whenever you know you feel that sense of hurt, disappointment, anger, or frustration. Here are some tips I personally use to determine whether or not my ego is perhaps slipping away a bit from the grasp of control..

Know Your Ego

Ask yourself the following questions, and be honest with yourself.

- *Do I get mad or envious of others?*
- *Do I let out negative or positive comments towards opinions first?*
- *Do I accept the ways the past has molded me?*
- *Am I nervous, or humbled by what I believe the future has to offer me?*

These four questions can help put the ego in check. It helps to put your perspectives in order, and what that organization allows for is clarity. That clarity, in turn, will help you make better decisions and ultimately reform the ego to a healthy balance of leveled self-esteem. If you continue to get mad or envious, it's because you feel entitled to something, ego. If you let out negative comments all of the time or even too many positive ones, either of those could be compensating for a threat to ego or lack of ego enough to insufficiently apply sustained confidence. If you accept the ways the past has molded you, the ego is silenced because you feel at peace with who you are. If you are humbled by what the future has to offer you, then you believe you deserve great things which is the sign of maturity because you no longer need the instant gratification. A person with sufficient confidence to continue on the path without giving in to other distractions is a person with the ego understood. When priorities become clear, you know its working. Not to say everyone is perfect, there will be times when we feel ourselves losing control, but the ability to bounce back and take ourselves out of our own head is where the power actually lies.

The Three E's – Expectations

"When you stop expecting people to be perfect, you can like them for who they are." -Donald Miller

Expectations come with contingencies. Meaning when you put hope on something or a story of what you think someone thinks of you, then your actions become less genuine and more as an act put on for others. Instead of you being a reflection of you at that point, you become a reflection of what others think you are. It's like that song by the award-winning hip-hop artist Eminem entitled "The Way I Am." In which he talks about being whatever people say he is. He says that if he wasn't, then why would it be said? Which is what we tell ourselves. We get it in our own head that we are whatever we tell ourselves that we are, all based on what we believe others think we should be. It is quite a phenomenon.

Realistically what we need to do is shut this out and completely block unhealthy expectations. I know that most say you need to overestimate your expectations to reach higher levels of success, but this is another version of that. This is the version where you exceed your potential by eliminating the values of others opinions. It is okay to value truth and validity of intelligence, but you are not required to take any views to heart, nor should you. When people praise you stay calm. When people judge you, stay calm. Remaining present while presenting unwavering courage will get you where you intended. Eventually.

Either way, this all takes hard work and dedication. Consistency with a combined level of enthusiasm for the whole process. Remember always to empower yourself and do not downgrade your thoughts or emotions. Become one with whom you are and really focus on your self-awareness. The most important and valuable thing you can bring to the world is your true self. The sooner we can grasp that concept and show as much compassion as we do complaints and negativity, the sooner the world will be off to becoming a much better place. Deploy insane amounts of empathy, and do not take things personally, audit yourself and begin to form your habits early. Be the change by first taking accountability and accepting the leadership role in your life. Once you let go, you take complete control, and that's what most strive for. Nobody ever has it all figured out but the ones that make it take the extra time to figure it out. All it takes is learning, growing, becoming more, and realizing that active patience is the key. Not instant gratification, nor unreasonable expectations brought on by ourselves or others.

The Three E's – Excuses

"Fortune favors the bold"

The Latin saying remains true. On the other side of fear is bliss. We're fearful of stepping up because it enters a new realm within us that is going to require exploration. We as humans are afraid of the unknown, so we create excuses, so we don't have to start. Do not overwork but know that work is required. This is why we need to grind in our early years and keep going with as much prep work as possible in whatever direction we're planning on going. What I mean is before you go crazy with working out you need to do a warm-up set to get the muscles working. I feel the same should go for us as well.

This is what usually sets the tone. People claim they have no time for this, they're too busy for that. When realistically, we all have the time to do anything we truly want to do. I completely understand that we've got to work plus go to school, on top of raising a family, so we make excuses as to why our aspirations are not getting done. All of these are valid reasons because you've justified them and made these decisions bind to your habits. Habits begin with words, but these are all just excuses that are too commonly used and have become an unconscious response due to lack of aggression. Every time your brain receives the stress signal, it immediately reverts back to the comfortability stage and hasn't been adequately trained to push the bounds on the will or unlock a deeper level of consciousness.

One of the ways you can negate these excuses before they occur is by taking accountability for everything around you. Kind of like when your parents used to say be honest, and the punishment wouldn't be as harsh or if much like pleading guilty and getting a lower sentence. The same concept applies. By taking ownership, you're already eliminating the excuse because you are no longer blaming anyone else for the lack of control in your own life. Think about it. The more responsibility and accountability you have for everything that happens to you, the sooner you have control over your emotional reactions. Suddenly when you get mad, it's because of you, not the end of the bed you stubbed your toe on last night.

Shift the blame immediately, so if you get upset, it's because of your own fault. As soon as you can let go of your pride and your ego, the easier this will be. Most people don't want to do the hard stuff, and most people also tend not to want to be honest with themselves. I know I wasn't honest with myself for so long! Yet, as soon as I started to make these changes, I noticed a dramatic change even in performance at work. When times would get hard, and I'd feel like quitting I'd remember that it may not be my fault as far as the circumstances, but it's entirely my fault if I continue to remain in this position. So I began to make shifts into the way I viewed work. Sort of making it my own without remorse. See, the beauty of taking responsibility for your own life means nobody and nothing can control you. It's insane how when you make this change, you instantly report to yourself and yourself only. At that point, this is when the accumulation of unknown regret can form. Excuses in the past, cause for habits in the present, which ultimately create disappointment in the future. Live a life of abundance, not a breath of excuses because what that will end up doing is leaving you with is an excuse for a living. Eliminate excuses!

We've got to set ourselves up for success, and one thing that is entailed is doing things we are unfamiliar with. Everybody is terrible at something they do for the first time. I bet you didn't stand up and walk the first time, did you? You were probably able to rise onto your own two feet but perhaps plopped right back down. I also bet you tried your hardest to keep getting back up. I bet maybe you cried or laughed and even though you knew you would continue to fall and fall, you also had unconscious faith that because others were able to do it with ease and normalcy, you eventually would too.

That very sense of self-belief is what strengthens who we are inside and keeps us striving. The same courage we display within ourselves and within our belief systems need to be consistently growing and adapting. Fear is a part of the journey. The difference in the people that gain any sort of happiness or success is that the ones with abundance are willing to dive into a deeper form of who they want to be. In turn, that allows them to overcome based on the perception that fears are the different levels of joy. The worse the fear, the higher the amount of pleasure that lies behind that curtain.

I always wondered when I was younger how all of the fancy businessmen could predict things and always seem to know what was going on with the market and could even relate it to simple tactics such as how to spend money and know when we're overspending. Even more so, how to use money logically to benefit the overall goal. The critical thing I never realized though was how much work I was not seeing to overcome the obstacles. It wasn't until a few years later that I would notice the fact that what I saw was just one glimpse. One small piece of a vast and well-orchestrated puzzle.

That's what I think we forget. The fear that we face at every turn is what leads up to success. It needs to become transformed into a pursuit of joy from within the courage we put forth. Not the inner courage we wish we could tap into. That, in essence, is the main villain, fear, at it again. However, now it comes as a manifestation of an excuse not to start or only to see the fear and not the bliss that awaits us. When we see the people, we look up to, or when we watch their videos, we only get a 5 second to 1-hour clip of a compilation of their lives. It isn't the times they are working or doubting, or even getting frustrated and becoming riddled with fear but pursuing the dream anyway. Those moments though, to me, are the things that make them who they are and what keep the good ones reasonable and what makes others great. The influence, however, is excuse built. If you really think about it, how do you think you may answer the following question?

If you had to choose, would you rather watch a 23-hour breakdown special on the day to day life of LeBron James as a regular person without any relation to basketball? Or would you rather watch the one-hour championship game against the Golden State Warriors? Most people would rather see the endpoint. Do not get your level one mixed up with someone's level 56. Life is a marathon, much as Jericho is about to find out. The sooner we can all focus on our race and not give in to the fear of thinking that we don't have the capabilities or the resources someone else has, the sooner we can all stop making excuses and start building our confidence. No matter the rubble, we should all be able to find faith.

Inflictions

"I no longer have any fear of pain because I'm the one inflicting it and can decide when it stops"
-Maude Julien

I think we've all experienced some level of negative self-worth where our past has led us to believe we are still that person. Or even worse, that the world would be a much better place without us. In turn, this can create self-doubt and eventually, self-sabotage. This is when our belief is so thwarted that we actually feel we are not worthy of good things, nor do we have faith that good things will come. We judge ourselves too harshly, and until we can learn to love ourselves completely and unconditionally, we will continue to sabotage our life and not feel as though we deserve it to get better.

What can stem from this is worry, more self-doubt, and negative talk, as well as more fear, distraction, and a damaged ego. These are breeding grounds for decision fatigue, more anxiety, stress, depression, or worse. In conclusion, though just remember that everything you're going through as far as hardship is only to further your progress. So start whatever it is that you want to do and begin to use progression to propel forward in the pursuit of that.

We need to learn to detach slowly. Not the detachment of yourself with others but with the stories we tell ourselves. The negative stories we add to random events which can spiral our emotions out of control. The universe gives us exactly what we ask for. So in turn, the things that happen to us along the way are formulated to be the tests we need to pass. The problem with this is that it's sustainable up until the point where we give them a story and a meaning behind it. This is why people react so differently to different things. Why some cannot worry so much. Perhaps it's because they know they've already taken steps to solve whatever problem is put forth and anything added on is just extra drama meant to test the growth so far.

Or maybe they simply know that they are the path and whatever they decided was meant to be. When we detach ourselves, we're able to take the wrong part of the ego out of the presence of the happening. Enough to be able to form our own truth and do the things we need to move the needle a bit. By detaching ourselves, we can also become more objective to situations and not as emotionally bound to what is going on

Do not get caught up in isolation. If we detach too much, this is when we begin to feel lonely. Loneliness and solitude are entirely different. Being separated is like being in solitude. When we are not auditing what we tell ourselves that is when isolation multiplies because we feel we are not worthy of what we desire enough to put that out to the world. That is also the exact moment when relationships are no longer authentic because now you're too focused on your own tunnel vision instead of the broader vision.

You will be able to start to see a shift in the fact that you are not genuinely having conversations, you are merely going through motions and becoming robotic. You begin to experience anxiety as opposed to optimism. This can be just as disastrous so stay alert in how much you are detaching your story with what is going on. If you begin to separate too much and begin to isolate yourself, you can always come back just start engaging more with others within your circle even if it's just a simple, but GENUINE, hey how's everything going? Social interaction will always trump being alone. Even scientists and psychologists have proven this time and time again with suicide rates linked to depression and overall levels of anxiety in today's modern world.

So be aware of these things. Remember that relationships are a part of this overall cycle. Always maintain the healthiest relationships possible with the ones that are encouraging and challenging you. Those are going to be the ones that will be able to get your out of the funk of isolation and back into the groove of detachment and ultimately one step closer to attacking any of those negative inflictions upon self.

The Mirror of Judgement

"Comparison is the thief of joy." -Theodore Roosevelt

So why do we continue to compare our lives to the success of others? That's what we are doing. We are seeing things we are taught to want only by societal standards. In addition to that, we base our level of success on a one hour Kardashian show, or a five-minute scroll through a motivational influencer feed on Instagram where it's all grind! Day in and day out, with actual time and resources to have professional pictures taken. Making videos to post all day while we all work and consume it. You take this as “All I've got to do is post a few pictures."

The fame we all see is fabricated. The money is a byproduct. That's what it's really about. Do any of us really want fame? I believe its admiration and some attention but not fame. Popularity comes with the openness of all aspects of life. Would you like to be stopped 51 times just to go to the airport because it's your fourth flight in three days and you are tired because you did this many events and had to talk to that many people? Not many people could remain poised enough to continue. Cultivate your fulfillment and begin to nurture it into reality.

This is what work does. The more work you do on yourself, the more of your fulfillment you can cultivate. Once you get that rush of unwavering happiness and courage, you will then be ready to nurture it into the vision you see for yourself. That's when everything comes full circle, and now this is an endless cycle of fulfillment, instead of an infinite sequence of dread. From the beginning now to the end where the beginning happens again. A Phoenix amid any sort of darkness you may be experiencing.

That is the real goal of this book to make everyone feel like they matter because you do matter. You do have something to contribute to society even if you think you don't. Also if your heart has been ripped out of your chest and you are lost, or if you have bipolar disorder or depression and have no control I want this system to work for you because it is something that I never had. I honestly never had anyone that could understand what I was going through, and I did not like the antidepressants. Nor do I like taking any sort of pills. Nobody should feel alone, and if you do you should not survive through the fear of judgment, but fully live through with the courage to be yourself and not apologize for it or feel you need to live up to a so-called 'expectation.'

Don't compare yourself with others. This takes away from your marathon. There's a picture of Michael Phelps that I had seen and will never forget. It was of him winning the 2012 Olympics, and you see Phelps looking forward about to win as his competitor has his head turned toward Michael.

It captivated me because everyone always seems to be doing this throughout life. Looking at other as they get ahead of us. Most people are ahead of you, though because they don't know who you are. What they pay attention to has everything to do with the future and absolutely nothing to do with what you're doing. This is the kind of mentality we should all possess because the way it works is once we compare ourselves we are taking away from the joy and the things that are in our lives.

Just like that, we instantly devalue our own self-worth without even realizing it. We pick up our phone and are instantly comparing our lives and being influenced that the basic necessities are material things or a life of luxury. Every successful person you have ever known will tell you to do what you do and compete with yourself. Obviously, take into account the trends and the market but do not for one-second envy what someone else has because if you truly wanted that particular thing you'd have it.

Indecisive Distraction

"I have wandered all my life, and I have also traveled; the difference between the two being this, that we wander for distraction, but we travel for fulfillment." -Hilaire Belloc

Distraction is one of those things where if you're not careful, you could be going down a path of indecision and confusion. One minute you may want this then the next you may wish to that and so on and so forth. During these moments, it is crucial to be self-aware of who you are. What are you good at? What are your real strengths and weaknesses? If you are a more visual learner, write them down on paper and begin to really analyze these. If you can take a step outside of yourself and answer your own fundamental questions, then you have already done most of the legwork.

Self-awareness is the most important thing you could do for your future self. This will create wisdom, and from that moment on, you will intake more knowledge. Similar to a liquid being poured into your soul. After you figure out who you are, the rest becomes clear. You will then pour out all of the abundances and put it out through your overflow. You first need to figure out what you love, not what you have always wanted to be when you grow up but what you actually enjoy. If you love basketball but cannot play, you can surround yourself with the environment and get lost in that passion. Once you find that the distractions minimize tremendously. You become so laser-focused on what you love that the other things become more obsolete. The goal ultimately is to have that passion become your purpose, but for now, just allowing yourself freedom in living based on what makes you feel alive is an exciting concept!

What happens when we don't become self-aware is that becomes the distraction. For example, how many times have you asked yourself what your purpose is? Who you want to be? Or what you want to do with your life? We focus more on those questions themselves then we do actually going about our days living out who we are.

Let's say you love bodybuilding and are good at it. You've won competitions and are doing well, but now you have this dream of aspiring to be the next Olympic swimmer. It's just not practical, why would you focus on things such as swim lessons and coaching and pouring the effort into that when you know you could do one arm 50 lb. Curl with perfect form! It's about identifying and creating something based off of the right variables. If you love bodybuilding that much, take more steps in furthering progression in that area.

Whether it be educating, writing books, starting a YouTube, anything. The sky's the limit! Don't let idle hands be your downfall in the discipline. People become distracted also when they start to judge themselves based on the people they are around. If people are doing well around you but you're not how do you take that? With a grain of salt or with a big ass boulder? Most times people feel as though they need what their friends have or what the people they look up to have because they don't know who they are. The influence around you will also cause for distraction.

Know who you are, know your ego, and be more willing to learn than yesterday. Even on a macro level, you will spend less money on frivolous things to compensate, and spend more time on the things that are going to change YOUR future individually. No matter what, above of all, you must figure out who you are. You may not fit in with anyone in your circle, you may feel alone like you don't belong. It isn't for the reasons you think, though. It will not feel that way once you open yourself up to who you indeed are inside.

Radiate who you are with the world and if it is just getting the news out or just painting a picture well then do that every day and revolve your life around that, not the job, not the bills, not anything that causes for distraction. If you saved all of the money you spent on the frivolous and only restricted it to what you need for what you love to do, then you would surprisingly have more clarity in your mind, more money, and more freedom because you get lost in certain aspects of it. The time you spend doing it, the way it makes you feel as you're doing it, and how proud you are of the progression you're seeing within your passion and as well as yourself.

The next day Jericho tried to replay the dream over in his head but to no avail. He soon went about his day as usual. There was more gratitude in his strut because of the amount of dehydration and agony the night prior, and also just kept having this feeling that it was more than just a dream. He was just that type of person, though, always questioning every little thing.

Perhaps it was just because growing up, he always was trying to figure out why his family was not better off. Not wanting to spend too much time contemplating everything, though, he did not want to be late for work. He ate breakfast and headed out the door to work. He now had a government job and was just pretty much working to keep the lights on. He got decent benefits, was able to save something from every paycheck and was off for the holidays, so it wasn't too bad for his lifestyle. He was bike riding routinely and consistently competing in marathons to maintain that sense of freedom for what he wanted to do.

So much of his childhood was based on things he HAD to do so, in essence, he just wanted to shift that paradigm. One day on his lunch break, he began scrolling through his YouTube feed to kill some time. As he was waiting for a video to upload, he saw an ad for an ultramarathon run. It wasn't so much the marathon itself nor the fact that it seemed excruciatingly intense that caught his attention. He'd had plenty of experience running them before. It was more so the location that had caught his eye… Without a second thought, he clicked on the ad and began reading the website description of the race. It read:

Atacama Crossing (Chile) 250 km / 155 mi, 6 -

Stage Ultramarathon

- **The course of the Atacama Crossing takes competitors across a wide variety of terrain in a 7-day race. Starting at just below 10,500 feet in the Arco Iris Valley, the race finishes in the quaint town of San Pedro de Atacama.**

- **Competitors will go through salt flats stretching as far as the eye can see, run down massive sand dunes which will literally take your breath away, go through canyons where you can touch the walls on both sides and sleep under glittering night skies in the driest place on earth.**

- **The course is varied. Sand-dunes, river crossings, gravel, loose rocks hard-packed earth and even waist high grass. This is in addition to the infamous salt flats that will challenge even the smartest runners to cross at full-speed.**

- **Each Stage of the Atacama Crossing has unique cultural, historical, and scenic highlights that will encourage competitors to push themselves along to the next checkpoint.**

- **The Atacama Crossing is a 155-mile running race. There are 6-stages in 7 days: almost 4 Marathons in 4 days, then a rest day and a final stage of roughly 7 miles.**

- **The Atacama Crossing race is self-supported, which means runners are required to carry all clothes,**

sleeping bag, necessary equipment, medical/safety kit, and 7 days of food in their pack. The race organizer only provides everyone with 2 to 5 gallons of water per day and tents for the nights. The goal is also to keep to the weight of the pack below 20 lbs., without water.

- **The temperature reaches as high as 115°F in the day and goes down to 43°F during the night. That means to bring more clothes. Also, the ground is rockier at the camps, so bring a mattress too.**

This was it! This was the dream! He was excited, startled, nervous, but sure that this was what it meant. He couldn't explain it. It felt as though it was all somehow connected. He sat back for a moment to really try and rationalize the inclusion he had come to. "I've got to do this," he finally exclaimed! The race was in 145 days. He began figuring things out and planning accordingly, filled out the form, and began preparing. He accepted the opportunity even though he wasn't sure why he was being called to do this. This could not just be a random coincidence, could it?

Part I: Mental Health & Gratitude

Stage One : Navigation by Rock

Jericho knew when getting on the plane that he was both totally thrilled and sick to his stomach. He was also fearful of the actual trek. Finally reaching such new heights and admittedly, was afraid of failure. He was worried that this would be something he may not finish, but that felt he needed to win at all costs! Amid the anxiety that was building, he also realized about halfway during the flight that either way, he would grow from this experience and as the thought deepened it was known that was all he really needed to focus on. At least to get him through this moment. He knew that even though he would be at the mercy of the lonely, dry, hot desert, still, there was a desire to take the challenge in full acceptance because he was never going to let the past define his ability to push the limits of even his own mind. Plus he would not make the same mistakes he had during previous marathons he'd run before. He would be thorough and strategic. Just as he had to be growing up.

He arrived at Camp Rio Grande - 10,518 Ft. above sea level. Live music was playing, people were dancing and laughing. He began to feel the butterflies within. "Nervousness means you care." his father always used to say. He always believed that there had to be 'more' to life, and this is precisely that more! At this point, he is fully confident in his abilities to carry this out to the end. He is in the right mindset. All of the limited beliefs growing up granted him a preparation and shaped it for this moment. He had to cultivate a mentality that would allow him to seek challenges as an opportunity as opposed to an obstacle as an excuse. His perspective from swift conversations with veteran runners was to focus on the beauty and not the finish. He was still trying to win, though.

As the runners line up. He is stumbling trying to hurry and finish getting ready, but he realizes that the bladder inside of his pack has busted. There was no time, they close the starting line off to people that do not check in within a specific time frame. He needed to take accountability, continue on, and keep pushing. Even if it meant risking more than he bargained for. He had to make a decision at that moment.

1. **Option one: Stop before starting, not wanting to jeopardize health. Or,**

2. **Option two: Start anyways and just figure it out as he goes along without any water until the next checkpoint?**

If you guessed option one, you'd be wrong. Playing back within Jericho's head again the saying he'd heard from his mother during his childhood, "be resourceful!" and that was his hope. Be as resourceful as he could. He was off, and so began the journey. Full acceptance, combined with well-primed cultivation of mindset, perspective, and accountability. For whatever possible outcome or obstacles may result from the events that were always meant to take place. Everything will always happen as it is supposed to.

Gratitude for Today

"Learn to be thankful for what you already have, while you pursue all that you want." - Jim Rohn.

Gratitude is something that is overlooked. One way to be able to identify if it is being overlooked is based upon the number of complaints either heard or made. Think about how many times you hear somebody say "I'm hungry" or "I want more money," or about where they are in life. That is usually the big one. A complaint stems from a state of being in the mind that is rather unwanted or undesired. The ability to gain perspective in these moments is the difference in which gratitude can become created, enhanced, depleted, or destroyed. Examples of extreme gratitude can go as far as being able to stay calm or motivated when things in totality are against you. When you jam your finger and do not get mad. It hurts yes, but you do not get angry at the door.

Have you ever noticed that many people that have the bare minimum or death-defying diseases are the most influential and some of the happiest people you will ever meet? Why is it that people knowingly closer to death are more at peace than those of us that take each second for granted? Some of the most wealthy and talented people taint their bodies and minds with alcohol, drugs, and spew negative influence while one inspiring story is never seen about someone achieving great success through impossible odds.

Gratitude allows for freedom. Not from your problems but from your attachment to this idea that anything can truly own your state of mind. When you become grateful, you will begin to notice a shift in what is essential versus what is irrelevant. This identification in priority can make all of the difference in the world for some.

For example, let's say you are late and are stuck in traffic or run out of gas on the freeway. You may get mad or upset, these emotions are healthy, but by merely identifying how grateful you are, you can increase the productivity in your reaction. So instead of getting mad and yelling and cursing at the car, you will take a breath, listen to your emotions, learn from what the mistake was or realize that things happen, and continue to take the steps necessary to take care of the problem because the fact of the matter is you are alive.

Being grateful for what you have is what allows you to be thankful for any future opportunities you wish to capitalize on. If you have running water but are ungrateful for it, the assumption is likely a belief that there will always be running water. Yet those same people are the ones that tend to get mad when the water gets shut off from a bill that is past due. That's the disconnection where people most often are ungrateful for what they have but want more money.

Being grateful for what you do have or the things money cannot buy means you're not focused on the money as an end result but more as a tool to help you get to that end result. The more grateful you are, the better the outlook of life becomes. It's simple logic. Let's say you are absolutely entitled and have all of the money in the world. You go your entire life getting anything you want with the snap of a finger. Then all of a sudden a bear market hits and you are left with no money, never worked a day in your life and no skills for anything. What do you do?

Believe it or not, there is a constant. On the outside, it seems as though all is lost, nothing seems practical because you are so distracted in your circumstance. No, you feel like a mess due to your own inability to see things for more than what they were, are and can be. This is where perspective comes in. Remember, in the preface, we discussed the idea of perspective and having the ability to see the pragmatic approach to the ways you should view things.

When you allow for both gratitude and perspective to flourish, you never feel left without. You feel empowered by what you do have at your disposal. When you can see just how unbalanced and just how unfair certain things are you realize that by taking accountability, you are now in control of your outlook. If your perspective is off, it's hard to see how to be grateful for the food on your plate. With the right idea of view and no gratitude, you will eat that food for nourishment but not be thankful for what it is providing for you. The two go hand in hand and to possess one without the other can leave you feeling just as unfulfilled as you already have. Be wary and mindful.

Become More Grateful:

Wake up every morning and say OUT LOUD what you are grateful for. Examples; A job, your breath, your family, your eyes, arms, legs, transportation, running water, sunlight, trees.

Write a list every morning of everything and read it OUT LOUD.

Think of things you could lose today that mean the most to you. (This will trigger an emotional response).

Put problems into perspective. (This will give empathy, issues are not secluded to you).

Let's view the same example used now, but with more perspective and gratitude added. You start off entitled, though your feelings are the opposite. You have all of the money in the world, but with gratitude, the difference is you are now not taking it for granted. The perspective that being grateful hands you is that of permanency. You begin to realize that your circumstances are not permanent, whether good or bad, so this allows you the freedom to continue through life as though you have no money, you can see both sides now.

This minor change can have life-altering effects because now when the bear market hits, you have had two ways in which you've prepared. One, you invested when the money was in abundance, so now you are ready and can even spend more on stocks because the pricing will be low.

Or two, you still lose the money, but the essence of your discipline is still intact. Since you were grateful enough to make connections and show you knew the value of your asset allocation, it will not be as hard for you to go about actualizing a more tangible fortune not obtained by inheritance.

Mindset Mayhem

"Gratitude is the healthiest of all human emotions. The more you express gratitude for what you have, the more likely you will have even more to express gratitude for." - Zig Ziglar

If you fill up a glass of water halfway is it half empty or half full? Well, it doesn't depend on if you poured it or drank it, but it does depend on how you think about it. A mindset is an established set of attitudes held by someone. There is either a growth mindset or a fixed mindset. Growth mindset is when you can see the gains over the loss or positive over the negative.

Not getting stuck in one way of thinking but knowing that we can all evolve, adapt, and become more than we are. A fixed mindset is when you feel stuck, plateaued like you are not moving and are only in a loss framework. It is essential to know these because, for the longest time, I had no idea I was in a fixed mindset. This hindered my potential to grow, and all I really ended up losing was time which is the most valuable asset you can lose but what I learned and gained from it all were a positive outlook and a refreshing growth mindset. I just want to be able to provide you with the same information I was dealt to further your knowledge and apply it how you feel the need to.

Negatives will last longer than positives, a study done by Psychologist Alison Ledgerwood provided evidence of this when she and a colleague provided an experiment in which they described, to its participants, a new surgical procedure that had been done.

They broke these participants down into two groups.

In group one, they described the procedure as having a 70% success rate. In group two, they described it as having a 30% failure rate. The same process, different focus.

People in group one obviously liked the odds of the 70% success rate procedure description more because it's put in a more positive frame.

Then they added a twist to it and told group one that another way they can think of it, is as a 30% failure rate, and decided to go against the procedure entirely.

Then told group two they can think of the same procedure as a 70% success rate and whereas the first group did, group two still did not change their mind at all.

This infers it is easy to get stuck in the loss frame of mind and not go back to gain. This is why people get so down on themselves whenever something goes wrong, and they fail. Failures take such a significant toll on the fixed mindset way of thinking and so if you are this type of person why it is so crucial to switch.

It is much easier to convert gains to losses than it is losses to gains, and it is this idea of being stuck in our own negatives that allows for people to stop growing perhaps without even realizing it. Negative is everywhere, and it takes the same amount of effort to push into a positive mind state, and more often than not people cease to continue the work it takes so they give in to all of the anguish and low levels of thinking.

Which is understandable given all of the celebrities and influencers posting only the filtered parts of life, all there is genuinely room for is comparison. We know what comparing ourselves does, so why do it? This is why it is so important to audit your language. People stick to the negative and believe it enough to let it consume their vocabulary and their thought process. If this is checked beforehand, you can help eliminate the complaints and the unwanted feelings of sorrow and begin to shift into training yourself on focusing on the upsides in those very same situations.

Most people do not like the idea of work but fail to understand that living a certain way takes a certain level of work ethic. Nothing is free, and freedom costs freedom of time. So how much would you be willing to sacrifice in the beginning to obtain more in the future? You cannot sacrifice more time than you have in a day, but you can sacrifice more freedom in the minutes you have in those hours.

Time will always be fixed and limited, so it's what you do in the hours that count. You cannot just sit and wait idly by as life continues to move. You must move with the current and learn to swim because if you are still on this earth, the fact of the matter is you still have to become what you were destined to be. We all have a purpose, and it's a matter of finding it, but the idea behind a growth mindset is your ability to overcome the short sided parts of situations and still be able to view it as an opportunity to extend what you have and not feel discouraged when you do not receive any sort of reward. Not feeling phased but somewhat challenged by obstacles and wanting to take the time necessary to move through the barriers.

What a growth mindset allows for is the ability to see the opportunity and challenge in things and to know that even the things that are fixed, such as time, for example, are instead leveraged to your advantage by squeezing every bit of opportunity out of what it is you're trying to do. It also allows for growth within ourselves because we no longer have fixed limitations on what we can and cannot do or become.

This is where you see people overcome addiction because you're able to overcome the mental framework of who you thought you were versus who you are trying to become. It means you don't become discouraged when things get tough but instead figure out a way to do it and if you fail having the ability to see the “L” as not a loss, but a lesson. When we can view it as a lesson, there becomes less judgment upon ourselves and more accountability for the amount of effort that wasn't being provided.

One of the first steps in owning your life is taking responsibility for the things that happen to you. We know that bad things happen and that unfortunate events occur but what we don't do is leverage that to our advantage and incredible amounts of opportunities to grow every day and become better than you were by 100%.

The Problem

The problem is most people are around fixed mindset formed individuals. This makes it very hard to break out of the social norms you are accustomed to. An excellent way to find this out is to realize that every conversation we are typically having is being predicated on others' lives, whether it be wishing or demeaning, then chances are those very same people complain or act better than people. Either way, that's a fixed way of thinking because there is no growth. Complainers complain, and if you fake being better than someone else, where will the growth occur? Unless you are switching to a growth mindset, you will always be fixed on what you don't have, which is being ungrateful and stuck in a loss frame of mind.

Next time something wrong happens, ask yourself what I can do with this opportunity? Next time you have time don't watch Netflix but instead, go for a workout or a walk, all of these examples show that when you grow, you flourish because you then are better every day. However, when you are fixed, you are fixed, which most people are. In fact, most of us feel as though we don't deserve it, or that we are not capable of even attempting making our dreams come true. What's not true is that statement though. Never believe you are not intelligent. The human potential is limitless, so begin to explore and grow and see just how far you can get.

What I've observed and learned is that we tell ourselves these stories around our deserving of things or our belief in receiving items. We don't think we have the capability, so we get stuck in the loss framework. Then all of a sudden, you hear yourself making excuses as to why you are not where you are or doing what you want to be doing. Not only that, but you also validate these excuses in your head, so they become faithful to you. Self-truth and self-belief are insanely powerful, and once you get caught up in that loop, the self-doubt starts to come in the moments you have opportunities to grow because that's what feels uncomfortable. So you get down on yourself because there's no point in trying and continue to make decisions based off of temporary comfort or relief. We are all trying to run away from something as opposed to running towards it, but the running towards it ensures change. The change provides becoming adaptable, and if you can adapt, you become adept. That will make cultivating a growth mindset much easier because you start to build small habits to progress into more prodigious formed habits that become situationally second nature.

What Is Success?

Before we even get to why let's ask what. What is your idea of success? Is it work-life balance, money, freedom, impact, followers, to be number one at a video game? Whatever it is you need to identify what this looks and feels like. What is it you want? This is hard for most people because most people, of course, want everything. The difference though see between you and the successful page you are browsing is they only want one thing, and that is to reach their potential and become better. Most successful people don't care about cars or clothes because it isn't about those things. Those material items are byproducts of their passions and the real reason why they do what they do.

What is your 'why'? This is something you'll hear in business and by motivators quite often but that is mostly because it applies to everything. The ‘why’ of what you're doing. A long time ago, I realized that the world simply didn't care about the personal problems I had. Also, it did it give any sort of guidance or achievable measurements of success. Instead, it just left feelings of anguish, impatience, envy, and so much rage. Mostly since there was this entitled notion, the world revolved around me. Selfish thinking I know, but I feel we all kind of have this feeling to belong, and I never belonged to any sort of crowd. Not a loner but just someone that wasn't interested in parties and who everyone was talking about in school.

Instead, I kept trying to figure out what kind of an impact I would make on this world someday, and it is in this belief my why was born. It is through the passion 'why' is born, and it is your need to want to better the world, even in the smallest way possible. Why do you wake up and do what you do? Kids? To pay the bills? To go to school and get a degree? Whatever it is somebody's counting on you to perform and execute, whether it's your family or your friends or even just yourself. It is incredibly vital to realize though that it just may not be in the ways you've always seen.

I always wanted to be able to help people in ways that I could, but I never even imagined I'd be writing a book on the very things I've had to get through. It all just happens the way that it happens, but you'll never know what kind of opportunities you could have if you simply just opened yourself up to change and adversity and realize that you do have something to offer that only you can. You do matter, and it's crucial to analyze your placement in society and find the purpose that helps others. A fixed mindset towards your dreams would be saying you cannot do it because there are already thousands of people doing that in your field. A growth mindset says yeah that may be so, but they realize that it hasn't been done through their perspective yet. I feel that's what people do is automatically devalue their viewpoint because they don't give themselves enough credit for the accomplishments they have received. There's a blurred line sometimes between being modest and just being totally and utterly judgmental so make this line a bit clearer because honestly if you been through some shit, then you've been through some shit. Don't sell it but talk about it. Own it.

Once you've defined why and decided what your journey is, you can begin to form your own definition of success. This is what manifests the vision into reality. You have to be specific in this approach and may be much harder than it sounds. You might find some days are harder than others, and that's okay because the truth is nobody is perfect, and perfection is an illusion. Once you've found your passion and are in the right mindset, you can start your building on your foundation! This is exciting because now nothing can deter you from your path and the finish line may be far, but at least there is one now as opposed to you watching on the sidelines or in the case of 2018, watching from your phone on your favorite celebrities Facebook feed.

This clarity in your belief is going to cause for massive action. The progression in stepping up in levels of thinking is going to become the measurement of growth. Many people have such a misconstrued opinion about money, and that net worth is the real measurement of growth, but it depends solely upon your definition of success. It also becomes the key in that visualization. To become self-aware, what are you good at? Employ all of the previous read pages, implement your why, and begin a sense of urgency to create your legacy. If you leave your families behind with something at least let that be it. Where do you see yourself in five years? That alongside your definition are the determining factors you need to commence the journey. For so long, the problems have been amplified in life and seemed as though the holes could never be climbed out of. Now the light at the end of the tunnel draws near, but keep in mind this is a glimmer of light. The purpose is much farther, but that is a good thing.

Fixed Mindset

In the same study, the fixed mindset is what the default is typical if you will. People automatically jump to negative as soon as it's presented because of the way our human psyche works. It just allows for an easier time going from gains to losses more than losses to profits. So it's being stuck in this sort of negative mind frame that doesn't give us the confidence necessary to succeed and grow in the ways we want. Then we become frozen by fear of failure and slowly but surely instead of doing, we do not even attempt to try. This is where dreams go to die, I believe. Remember to make mistakes as lessons, and fail often. There is so much time left, and forgetting to take all of the opportunities to fail simply means having nothing to regret.

The idea of progression is using any positive momentum to push you forward. In any aspect of life. Don't let one person tell you they didn't like your story, and so you stop writing forever. Say you love writing, but nobody reads any of your work, do not let that deter you from pursuing your dreams. No matter what you do, it is imperative that you find your passion and dive into it without thinking about anything else other than the joy and happiness that it brings you. Form a relentless growth mindset to pursue the dreams you otherwise wouldn't. Fixed mindsets only let you fit into a box so big. Don't be forced to conform just because you were told it was right. Begin to break the barriers of what is fixed and what is allowing you to evolve into much more.

Another study done by Dr. Carol S. Dweck, a psychology professor from Stanford University, involved ten-year-olds and experimenting with her 'Not Yet' approach to progression and mindset. She gave students some challenging problems that some thought was a good challenge, and that others thought were too hard, even admitted to looking and comparing themselves to the other students that did worse than them to make them feel better, or also go as far as cheating the next time.

The fixed mindset as I'm sure you guessed is that of the students that simply did not accept the challenge as wholeheartedly as the others. It is the idea of praising the progression and the process of trying new things that allow for the momentum to build. Now can you guess which did better? Yes, you are correct! Of course, the growth mindset students did much better, but it may not be for the reasons you think. It may seem as though there are just certain people with this growth mindset ability, and for others, it is non-existent. Well, that just is not true. In this same study, the students that were given praise and taught the growth mindset showed more neurons firing in the brains and creating new connections of learning, and they were actively becoming smarter. The same students that weren't taught the same mindset showed steadily declining results. Change the way you think about difficulty and challenge. Start isolating when you are showing progress and praise it.

Learn to embrace more because the more adversity you face, the better you become, and that is on a moment to moment basis, so take every opportunity. Put more effort into every day, and every day will put more growth in front of you. It all comes down to your choices, you need to make the decision to be happy and to overcome any challenges first thing when you wake up. In the morning, when you first snooze your alarm clock remember, say out loud, "No matter what happens today, I choose to be happy and to overcome anything in my way." Now you get up and begin your morning routine.

We've got to watch the way we think and the decisions and choices that come before. Think of a never-ending loop much like the water cycle in which thoughts turn into words, seep into action, that action then grows into habits, those habits form interest which represents our actions over time, which then compounds to the point where we justify and always reform these choices, becoming more fixated on limitation rather than possibility. The steps we take are our choices, and we choose based upon that which we think. Which is why it's so crucial to audit what you listen to, read, and overall consume on a second to second basis. You've got to always be on guard at the doorway of the mind.

So ask yourself what is going right in my life? We never ask that question. We are always so quick to spew out the negative and the bad and complain about this and that but what went right today? What are you happy about instead of talking about all the things you are mad about? Shift away from the negative altogether and write a gratitude journal, practice rehearsing the good news instead of the bad news, and every time you feel the need to complain just think about everything that you have accomplished. We all take less and less time for ourselves because we are continually feeling pulled to help others and be there for others but truthfully you cannot help anyone if you are the becoming the addition to the problem. Take a step back and figure out which one you are and become more fixated on having a stronger growth mindset.

Pile On Perspective

"Every day stand guard at the door of your mind" - Jim Rohn

If you were to create a list of things that are keeping you from achieving your dreams, what would it look like? What would be on it? Would it be items such as expenses, debt, overhead cost, startup money, and people not helping? Well, regardless of what is on that list, what I can tell you is this, much like division, there is one common denomination that is hidden underneath all of the above notions. Have you figured it out? I will give you a hint, it is absolutely not anything that you listed above. If you guessed yourself, then you guessed correctly. One way is to look at it with perspective. Everyone is affected by everything.

The wind blows on everyone, the rain pours on everyone. However, it is in this idea of perspective, you can identify that even though times are hard, they are not permanent. Just as we use our growth mindset, we view our circumstance as an opportunity to overcome the new challenge. Realistically this isn't Jupiter with a storm cloud raging on for hundreds of years, the amount of wind usually surpasses, and until then you figure a way to adjust your sails. Much as it will not keep raining but if it does, you buy an umbrella.

The point is that we can evolve and flip anything to our advantage. Leverage is such an incredible trait to have. Nothing is permanent, and any idea of growth automatically instills a belief of change. Begin to honestly believe that the power of change and growth through progression is real, and it can propel the recognition of the fact that it is truly about the journey and not the destination. You have the power to create your problems, but the absolute beauty of that is that you are also the solution to every single one as well. It's a problem waiting to be solved. Figure it out.

Part of having good character means doing what you need to every day because you need to, not want to but need to. It's when you turn the want and should do, into can and will do. That's when things will start to shift. People often get confused between desire and need. People want externalized things, but what I've found is the more wants you have externally, means the more needs you are deprived of internally. So what are these needs, well the basic human needs are water, clothes, shelter. While the other spiritual needs a person is awaiting fulfillment on may be one of the six needs in which the extraordinary motivator, Tony Robbins, states are clarity, variety, growth, connection, significance, and giving beyond ourselves. The clarity in what is to come. Variety, in that we feel we need something different, growth in that we always in some form crave the need to grow, connection to other people, so there is less loneliness, significance so we can feel like we carry something vital and unique, and giving back because we as humans are built to serve some kind of purpose. A sense of belonging to something. An approval if you will. Chances are you were attempting to gain acceptance from one of your parent's mother or father in an attempt at perfection or behaving a certain way or living a particular lifestyle. If this was not you, then you are similar to myself in which I always tried at acceptance from other people. The craving of wanting to make an impact and fulfilling these needs is why there are so many social media stars.

The successful ones have found a way to provide value in some way to a mass group of people. Even if it's something that you or I am not necessarily into, you better believe there is still a niche out there for it. Even with all of that being said, however, just take note that you need to be better and undertaking something new is normal but the ones that pursue their dreams have a sort of self-discipline in doing what they are passionate about. So experiment with everything you can and try to find what makes you the best at being yourself. Then hone in on that and enjoy every minute. Become more internally sound having a good foundation set, and I guarantee the less the external factors will play a part in how you live every day.

The beauty of all of this is the fact that you are learning it now. You still have so much time to leverage what you can and become or create that life you always wanted! What's stopping you? Opinions, your fixed mindset, the negative network of people around you, the excuses? Realistically the only thing stopping you is yourself. Everyone experiences self-doubt, and everyone experiences the same fears.

Everyone has the same amount of seconds in the day to get the same level of effort put forth. The only difference is some wake up like myself and three o'clock in the morning every single day with ambition and excitement knowing that I have been blessed with yet another opportunity to be more than I was yesterday. I implore you to practice having a growth mindset if not for you then for the people around you because if you are not doing it, chances are you are the anchor holding everyone else down. You can have the tallest building one of two ways, by building others up or tearing others down. Be the bigger person and show how strong and evolved you're becoming. Which will you choose to do? How will you be remembered? For helping or for hurting?

Leverage

So if I say, life is picking on you, how do you take that? As being bullied or as you being called upon? That's the difference that is making or breaking your self-esteem. Some people believe life is happening to them and not for them, so they become insecure about their decisions and even intentions. They don't realize that the power they want to have lies inside of the journey they do not wish to undergo. Do you remember playing video games and to get past certain stages, you'd have to go through the lower levels all the way through to get a key or something that you would not have found otherwise? Life works very similarly. Let me explain, see to get the key to a new door you'll have to go through a journey to find it. In the life aspect it could be a sign you notice or a coincidence or even perhaps the whole right time right place scenario but as soon as you're able to see what stands out in particular moments follow that and see where it takes you. This concept is beautifully explained and utilized through contextualized examples in the famous book entitled The Alchemist by Paulo Coelho.

Life happens for you. If you always have it in the back if your mind that failure is going to be the outcome well then you've already depleted your belief. You've got to change the narrative and change the mindset. You've got to retell this story to yourself and begin to feel what you believe can actually happen. The reason so many people are not successful is that they fail to believe in themselves, and they don't love themselves enough to try and work at becoming better. They settle, and that allows for inconsistency. Consistency is paramount in growth. Imagination is a beautiful thing, and life can be too if you allow yourself to open up to it. Dreams can only stay dreams for so long. To shift this mindset and have the reality of abundance is to be accountable for both the problems and the solutions. It isn't enough to work hard for results. You must also gain reward in the effort as well. Treat yourself, give yourself a pat on the back for even making the decisions that are hard for you. Too often, we listen to our ego and allow it the luxury of deciding on what is okay or not. We give it too much strength instead of silencing it and allowing our true, divine self to respond in these moments instead.

One way to actively stimulate this shift in brain chemistry and provide the feel-good levels to spike naturally would be an increase in physical activity. This one plays a significant role in most people's lives. Nobody wants to get into action, but they don't realize that it's the lack of work that has gotten them to this point. The one constant to take away is starting the change. Most people put so much off until tomorrow and then all of a sudden five years go by, and that person, all of a sudden, hates the way they look in the mirror. Sometimes we get so used to ourselves each day and so we don't physically see a transformation happening. Much how if you haven't seen someone for a long time you will notice the first few things that have changed physically about that person. Don't get caught up in the day to days, instead embrace the day to days and make the most out of them because the truth is if you make the most out of today well then you make the most out of your life and there really is no comparison to that.

Remember to make marginal adjustments to your habits it doesn't have to be this drastic change. Remember to reward your efforts and your decision also, more so than the end result. Remember to use your hands to help with what you can do, remember to use your head to think about how to become better, and use your heart to love unconditionally. See the good in humanity because it is there. Beneath all of the benign bullshit that we've all become much too familiar with. Remember to be mindful of your emotions and the ways you feel. Remember to forgive yourself if you fail at trying to better yourself because the fact of it all is that you will fail. You will fail, but with every failure, you will have a choice.

You can both get back up and try again, or you can stay down and begin to reach comfortability. One thing I can tell you from personal experience and keen observation is that growth weighs more than mistakes. Not in stress weight but in actual weight. Growth is like training to lift the more significant pressure to get as healthy as you possibly can. Mistakes are like the warm-up reps. You must get yourself, much like your muscles, used to what it is about to do. If you simply go straight for the heavyweight, well several things could go wrong. The same could be applied through life.

Nothing is more important than our ability to optimize and become better than what we are. As a species, we thrive and live for purpose and meaning. Whether it be selfishly or selflessly. Either way though the idea that becoming better beyond what you see for yourself is excitement enough.

Small Adjustments

When we avoid things, it's because we don't believe we have the capabilities of getting through the situation we're avoiding up front. It's also because we're not honest with ourselves about what we want, so we feel we can justify making do with the way things are. This was me for the longest time. It wasn't until I decided to take the reins and have control little by little, and slowly but surely little things began to improve. Personal relationships have been strengthened, and new is forming. Along with more ideas coming into alignment with reality in what I always saw as my vision, it's been quite overwhelming, to say the least, to think that all it does take are little adjustments.

Much like our diets, weightlifting, losing weight, or saving money, we all need to make small adjustments for the significant overall increase. This also teaches an active sense of patience as well and is good at getting you to feel confident about the goal in totality. You can't expect to lose all of the weight you want by exercising one time

Takeaways

- Small adjustments compound over time.
- You can analytically view progress reports.
- You will see and get results. This will develop better habits daily in the process, becoming a lifelong learner.

These small adjustments also compound over time. Which means as these minor tweaks begin to form, they multiply as they go. Then again, and again. Until eventually, you are left with different forms of self-mastery. That's what investing does in the market, and that's how it works with your self-development. Your traits will multiply over time, and money will amplify it in addition to that as well. So if you're a lazy person with no energy and isn't eating right, chances are that you will only get worse as the years fast forward and if you did come into a fortune it would further project itself into food or luxurious depreciated assets as opposed to becoming an investor or even paying for a gym membership. If this person did, in fact, want to get into shape, it is highly likely that they will probably be at it for a week and feel it isn't working how the infomercial described, so they stop. This is just how we are as humans. We have this unique desire to serve beyond ourselves, yet we want instant gratification so severely. It's no wonder people view social media as a threat.

Instant Gratification

People don't understand that switch that tells you nothing earned is instant. Let me repeat that NOTHING EARNED IS INSTANT! Get that into your head right now. The sooner you can realize this the more patient you can become and know that whatever you are going through is not permanent if you have the willingness enough to do something about it and take immediate massive action to further yourself as far as you can go today so that it compounds into the future. I always was left wondering how people I used to go to school with would seem to be so well off and why I still struggled. For one, I realize it was me in part comparing my life with others and thinking that I wanted what they wanted.

Also though I realized that it was because they would do these small things like save here and there or get a certificate something, and all of the sudden they had a new car and a better job. It was always hard to grasp. How can I stop living paycheck to paycheck? Then it hit me, and I began doing this with everything. You do the work now for the results later. Or you can have effects now and work then. Which would you rather have at the end of your life? I'll take results later, please. If you can do the 20% of work on the right things in life and figure out what they are, isolate and attack. Then you will get the other 80% back with that in full compounded over time. It all depends on what you put in and how much you're willing to invest after that.

You can also view your progress throughout. As opposed to seeing a massive gap from 0 to a million. You will see which marginal adjustments to make. It goes back to the pragmatic approach and being trial and error. You need to fail if you want to succeed. Why is that though? Sounds unfair but it's because there's no rulebook. Think about this, there are so many ways to become successful that nobody can make a guide for it because everybody and their failures are different. The difference between you and the successful people is that they didn't see anything as a failure they saw them as marginal adjustments to work on and continue to learn from to further themselves and better their career or lifestyle choices.

As a child, most kids would hide their progress reports, and I always used to assure my parents that if it was terrible, it wasn't anything to worry about because I knew exactly the amount of work required to further the grade the way I wanted. I do remember my science class being kind of boring, so I didn't exactly pay attention, and so my progress report showed a complete F I believe of about 56%. I wasn't fazed, but my parents were. I assured them the grade would be higher come midterm assessments and they entrusted in me to do so, as I did to avail! I finished that first semester with a 94% I believe, and this was just in time for Christmas! Sometimes all it takes is knowing where you are so that you can make a baseline and go from there to begin tracking your progress via notes or journal, video, audio, social media. As long as it is recorded so you can view it or hear it and not just use your own ego or self-doubt to be the judges of these.

The small adjustments are what matter and you can plan for tomorrow as much as you'd like, but the essence of it all is that you only have today. You only have this moment, and you only have what is in front of you. You can make decisions based on a future event you wish to happen, but the only thing that could possibly guarantee that is your ethics. Your ability to touch the line and stay disciplined enough to love your potential and reach as far as you can. So many have not figured out that there is no rule book. There are no guidelines. There are success stories, and there are a million ways to go about things in today's society.

It all comes down to your work and what you can provide for the market, and it also comes down to your ability to network and meet different people. Once you've built and once you've saved some money, everything starts to fall into place. Once you've found your true passion and purpose. If you haven't yet don't worry. It will take time and experimentation in different areas to really get this down. Once you find it though you know you are on your way.

Accountability Is Control

"You cannot escape the responsibility of tomorrow by evading it today." - Abraham Lincoln

From what I've noticed, so many people feel ashamed of their faults, shortcomings, and even their problems. Yes, issues, people feel as though they should be ashamed of what is creating them. It is entirely understandable that if you are a drug addict or have trouble holding a job or even have trouble connecting with people that you may tend to feel ashamed because the problem is what has been holding you back for so long.

I felt so ashamed of my problems. I never opened up about them to anyone. When I lost up to five family members in two years, I withdrew and suppressed many emotions, and when it came to school, I was ashamed to tell people about the problems of my home life. Only being able to afford so much, and having my parents be the most gracious people I know but being hindered themselves by exposure and environment. Hitting plateaus early, which resulted in abuse of alcohol, medication, and drugs along with domestic disputes and many arguments stemming from insecurities formed long before. Then going about life working, going to school, and playing basketball.

During this period, I was extremely introverted and would eat lunch alone because I wanted to. I never felt connected with anyone. This led to feelings of such shame later in life. Skip a decade then, and at 26 it took its toll when I began to resort to addiction in different forms and would sabotage my life based on the fact that I was depressed and unsatisfied with who I was even though I was masking the fact that I was unhappy. This compounded over time, and everything blew up.

The change happened after the explosion. Once I realized what I was losing. When I decided that everything had been my fault from the very beginning I was able to take that accountability and build momentum into who I knew I wanted to become. I stopped blaming my parents for the way that I was and started thanking them for what I am becoming. It is our struggle that makes us who we are, whether you like it or not the worst problems we face turn out to be our most important stories of success. That's because on the other side of fear is your deepest desires. It is such a scary thing to take on the situation we're most afraid of, but when was the last time you faced a fear and something terrible happened? Think about it. Discomfort is the best gift you can give your future self. That adversity is what allows up to grow, and without it, we have no sense of progression.

Do not blame anyone for your situation. Don't wait until you are facing the compounded problems that have multiplied over the years. Instead, remember that the good habits you learn and develop early will always extend and amplify as you keep building. So don't stop moving and keep being responsible for what happens to you. It's when you release every one of fault that you become free and everything that happens to you at that point you can now have control over. You've got to take pride in the things that you've accomplished and continue to further yourself every single day.

There is not one day that goes by that we all do not think about our death in some form. You get scared of things because you feel they will affect your life. We are so driven by fear instead of taking the offensive and having the power of accountability to handle any of the problems in your life currently. Treat these issues as a CEO would. Obviously, everything is connected so instead of cowering and dreading the bills, think about making scheduled payments or maybe even negotiated an arrangement and actually taking the initiative to take control of the situation by letting things fall as they may and picking up the pieces to rebuild.

I remember all of the years I was in Sales I basically would diffuse other situations with angry customers and handle it by doing the same thing, taking responsibility and really listening to the problem. Letting the pieces fall and letting them get out what they needed to but fully explained the situation and calmly issued a quick compromise. Most often it's misunderstanding and a lack of someone to blame. Most people don't want to be blamed but instead, want to do the blaming. Once you take this blame and own it, this assumes that part out of the entire conversation. At that point, the focus is not whose fault it is but rather who can fix it and how? And as we've discussed before the power of being a problem solver is real.

Stand Guard

It is essential to realize that not all thoughts are right. I'm sure you've had more experience with that than you care to count, but the idea is that those negative thoughts and beliefs were able to seep in. It's healthy, but this is where the disconnect happens. Most people feel like they need to intake these negative thoughts and either push them down or "overcome" them but remember, the idea is to transfer that energy into something productive and positive.

It is imperative that you do this because it could make

or break the amount of time you waste sulking and making excuses for not doing what you want to be doing, or why you are not where you want to be yet in life. You've got to remember to stand guard and offensively attack these negatives before they hit the doorway. There could also be disguised positives too that look just like negatives, and this is why meditation is an excellent tool to have in the old tool belt.

You can be mindfully aware of your surroundings, as well as your emotions and figure out which thoughts are affecting which areas in your life. Everything just becomes simpler to associate and identify. So now you have more of a foundation as a whole, and you can begin to steer the energy into the directions you desire opposed to the other way around. Always remember that to surrender control gives you complete control.

Sage 1 is a trek that takes competitors through the multicolored 'Valle Arcoiris' (Rainbow Valley) and along 'Ancient Inca Road' where there is ancient rock art from the Inca and Aymara traders that were used in ancient times. He recalled the same formations within his dream and just admired it all with complete presence. There was no fighting the urge to quit aside from sticking one foot in front of the other regardless of the thirst. He hadn't had water since the very start of the race and was definitely experiencing all of the side effects. Though all he was hearing were the whispers his own self-doubt, he quickly created a loop of remembrance in which he combats those negative talks. With more faith and gratitude, that was what was able to kick in gear and allow him the strength to keep going. Just as the faith did when he was a kid trying to be better for his family. Things worked out then, so if he put forth the same amount of effort towards this, then it will happen again!

As he regained some perspective, his mind began to wonder. There were so many people gathered for one purpose, and it was all to enjoy it. Could that be the bigger picture? That is the question he couldn't help but keep asking. He thought, maybe it isn't so much about the race but about the entire journey collectively as a whole. Coming together to simply challenge, laugh, and enjoy themselves on the way. So many realizations on the opening few miles. Jericho was still riveted with excitement. It could be equated to the time he got his first bike back during that one memorable Christmas long ago.

As he came out of the Valley, he also came out to complete openness. Just miles of beautiful, sandy terrain with absolutely no shade, no wind, and no sound. Only the breath of himself and other runners around him trucking and enjoying the views and the beauty. It was as if he had Deja vu from the beginning of the dream that night. "This is where I'm meant to be," he reminded himself just as he reached the first checkpoint almost 22 miles later, he felt this overwhelming sense of calmness come over his entire body. He now reached a new level of gratitude, becoming more aware and well versed in his mental state than he ever had before! Stage one complete.

Part II: Physical Health & Momentum

Stage Two: The Slot Canyons

Jericho embraced his newly formed level of gratitude and was able to enjoy every step truly. Though he had many doubts and although he had begun with no water, he didn't just give up and not start. Instead took accountability and gained a new level of perspective in the process. All while reflecting upon the worth he had once perceived was his, versus the newly cultivated belief. Which, in turn, allowed him to finish and have such a less fixed mindset about the next leg. He grew a little, through all of the fear, pain and his own inflicted self-sabotage due to the made-up stories he was telling himself. It's a good thing too because what he is definitely going to need going into the canyons, is some momentum.

Stage 2 ensures that no feet are left dry, but takes competitors along the most stunning narrow, deep and scenic canyons, carved into the floor of the valley due to flooding thousands of years ago. After rising up a steep hill, you hit several breath-taking sand dunes that feel like clouds as your shoes begin to sink beneath the surface. The patterns themselves, however, allow for magnificent views across the plains while descending into the famous Valle de la Muerte (Valley of Death).

Momentum for Tomorrow

"Self-discipline is self-love." - Will Smith

According to Alzheimer's Disease International, someone in the world develops dementia every three seconds. There was nearly 46.8 million people diagnosed in 2015, almost 50 million in 2017, and this number is expected to double every couple of decades. At this rate, 75 million people in 2030, and 131.5 million in 2050. 58% of these people all come from lower-income countries and classes. That percentage is predicted to increase to 68% by 2050. People are already at such a disadvantage and yet they don't even know it. Science Daily posted an article on June 28, 2018, stating that healthy aging combined with obesity has a higher risk of this disease also. Half of it deals with genetics and aging, the other half is lifestyle choices.

Now that we've got those crazy statistics out of the way let's move how to set up these routines for you and how to set aside your hour blocks so that you productively plan your days and morning to set you up for success

The beginning to any type of fulfilled life is going first make changes to what you eat, and just overall health so be sure to develop a light workout plan even three days a week just to help keep yourself and your body in check. Also, it never hurts and helps with discipline if you can develop these healthy habits early on because you're less likely to make rash emotionally crippling decisions because you will have already gained the knowledge of how to go about creating a fulfilled life for yourself. It's fine to go to that party and chill and have a beer but be mindful that what you put into your body will compound the later you realize just what is going on with all of these choices. It is not easy but starts with eating.

Believe me, I used to be the pickiest person when it came to food. I wouldn't touch or eat anything that had a unique texture. Not sure but for some reason, it just indeed invoked my gag reflex and I would more often than not either pound it back with some water just to get it down or basically spit it all out. It was until about a year and a half ago when I would go work out with one of my good friends, and in aspiring to become a trainer he would be filling my head with what I had yet to realize was the foundation for my start.

So once I realized that after between 25-30, our organ reserve, as well as muscle deterioration, would accelerate at the rate, it would be currently, during those five years of life. This is what propelled me to take the leap. I made small changes such as intermittent fasting and trying to experiment with foods that I could tolerate. It is always so misconstrued that you need to dive right into every dietary plan readily available to you and as soon as it fails, mostly due to not even knowing what you need, you immediately blame the diet. If this is you do not worry, it's not because your body is uniquely formed to counteract all foods. It's because you don't know what you need precisely.

It is ALWAYS best to go see an actual doctor to get a baseline of what the chemical makeup of your body is. Start using apps to keep track of everything you eat to see what exactly your high and low levels may be. I write this because I do realize some of the people reading this may not have the luxuries of health insurance so until you can get it or figure something out do what you can and keep track of something! I can say that most people do get too much sodium in their diet as well as carbs. These two in combination alone with simple sugars can cause for a very unhealthy gut biome, which can dictate even your personality.

It isn't entirely our fault. The world has tricked us into thinking we need that burger, or we need that ice cream, and of course, business is business after all, and will always be business so you can't expect it all to all be healthy for us. People need to make money, and for some, the value of money does trump the importance of ethics. However, we were born with this crazy thing called 'will' and it allows us the freedom of choice. So choose the things you know you need to, not for yourself, but for the cells inside your body. Just like we need to grow, our cells also need to, and it is our job to give it the nourishment it needs whenever it feels depleted. You wouldn't pour dirty oil or water down your car to make it run a few more miles, so don't do the same with your body. It is up to us to take care of our bodies, and it all begins with what we put inside of it.

One thing many doctors will never argue with is to begin switching to as many whole foods, and vegetables as you can. However, do be careful because certain starchy vegetables such as broccoli and corn have different effects on the body so do some research or get seen by a medical professional to truly begin to take the right steps in adjusting your plan accordingly. It seems like a crazy amount of work, but trust me when I say when you get it down, it becomes a habit and more effortless to the brain.

Self-Discipline

"Discipline is faith in action" - Russell Brand

Self-discipline is what separates the good from the great. The ordinary citizens from the superheroes themselves, the ones that stand above all of the rest. Or at least the ones that rise above the majority. People misconstrue self-discipline and feel as though it is a form of punishment against something. When in reality, it is when you love yourself. It changes your mindset and starts to shift into what you should be doing versus what is actually being done. When people think of punishment, they tend to rebel at the fact that they are acting in their own self-interest and instead do the opposite of what they should be. Whereas if it stems from a place of love, then you are more susceptible to doing it because you are acting in your own best interest. Not to say everyone else falls to the wayside I simply mean in the good of your future self. You cannot spread yourself so thin that you become too fragile. You must still maintain a level of consistency as not to break by the weight of certain aspects in life.

One way to combat this idea of rebellion is by having a routine you follow every day that allows the use of better decision making, and overall use of the brain in general. In addition to that, feed your mind and beginning to invest in future habits that ultimately aid your formation instead of deleting it. The first and last hours of the day are vital to this. Most people scramble the previous hour trying to get everything done on time and in bed, so they do not even plan for the next day. Nor do they give themselves an hour minimum with ten minutes in between that to prime for the day and prepare for the challenges that lie ahead.

The brain is only capable of making a certain number of right decisions a day. Typically at this point, my only choice when I wake up is happiness. This is why people such as mark Mark Zuckerberg or Bill Gates wear simple, bland clothing and often the same clothes every day mostly because they do not want to waste time making decisions that have no impact on their goals for the future. So don't waste any ideas or judgments and instead try to perfect a routine that works for you. In the example of fitness, muscle fibers are torn during weight training, and during the resting period is when they rebuild, becoming more prominent and stronger. The same works for the brain. It is just as essential to get quality rest as it is to work out the mind in itself.

This means be vigilant in your pursuit for greatness but also stand guard and know when it is time to take a second to breathe and rest your mind so that it can grow. So adequate quality rest is vital. I know people say things like "Grind all day hustle all night," or "I don't get tired," but the truth is we all get tired. It's a natural human function. Most dementia in Alzheimer's cases are linked to sleep deprivation than any other disease, and that scares the living crap out of me! It should scare you too.

Do not feel bad when you need a nap. It is perfectly fine to do so. In fact, studies show that it is better to take a midday nap, as is shown to produce more overall productivity, than not taking one. Most of us do not get a full 8 hours of sleep, and at least one hour of it is us tossing and turning trying to get into a deep sleep. When people tell you not to take naps though because you're hindering your growth, just remember the fact about one of the worst diseases in this world.

Touch the Line

When I used to play basketball beginning from kindergarten all the way through to high school, there was this saying we went by when we would run called "touch the line." This meant that every time we would do sprints or ladders or down and backs we would have, or we had to start over. Needless to say, there would always be someone not touching the line, and we would have to run it over, and over, and over and over again!

This is why I do feel sports are so crucial to the ways we think about things and get us to push through our own boundaries. However, it was through that practice that I developed that way of thinking and started applying it to my own life. I would find myself "touching the line" so to speak in everything that I did whether it be homework, working out, basketball, work, or just at home I would always be going my hardest and always putting it all out in the flow touching that line and not making any excuses as to why I didn't.

For me, it has always been if you want to live like the one percent, you've got to be willing to do what 99% of people are not willing to do. I do realize though that this is much easier said than done. Majority talk a fair game, but when it actually comes time to put a plan into action for some reason, everything gets tensed up, and it becomes difficult to see the big picture anymore. Everyone attempting at bettering themselves has gone through a similar issue. One thing to note is by taking the levels necessary you will encounter the same problems others in your position have faced, but just by even showing up, you are doing most of the work in itself. The other part is applying the knowledge you've gained and continue to learn in your field or whatever it is you are interested in. It is essential also to note that you realize happiness is ultimately your journey throughout, in its entirety, not just the end result. The end result to be quite honest is death.

This is why a growth mindset is imperative, so the ability to take the losses as wins, and failing with enthusiasm is coherent. Enough to take on the daily challenges faced in life without deterring from the path of growth and progression. It is so easy to become discouraged either from people or our own self-doubts to the point where they cripple our decisions but don't fall for that fear-based thought process. Instead, just realize that who you are is who you are, so don't let anybody make you feel less for that. If they do, well then simply proceed with the elimination of that very person promptly!

Clarity and Focus

"It's the repetition of affirmations that leads to belief. And once that belief becomes a deep conviction, things begin to happen." - Muhammad Ali

It's easier said than done just to produce useful energy from bad trust me, I know, but this is why we all need all of the help we can get. It isn't enough to just feel positive. We need to start taking advantage of everything we have at our disposal, instead of taking for granted the bodies in which we have to thrive. We are what we eat, and I feel people genuinely do not understand the crisis we face with obesity and unhealthy compounding habits.

Basically, we are taking the junk and trying to turn it into fuel that will allow us to perform. The worst part is most people are not willing to take the time to genuinely care about themselves and end up waiting until it is too late. Others simply don't care, and others just feel it is too expensive. A palliative nurse recorded the top five regrets of people on their deathbeds and put it into a book entitled "The Top Five Regrets of Dying." This was the list she shared.

1. I wish I had the courage to live a life true to myself.
2. I wish I hadn't worked so hard.
3. I wish I'd had the courage to express my feelings.
4. I wish I had stayed in touch with my friends.
5. I wish that I had let myself be happier

Do not wait until it is too late. Take care of our bodies

now, and our bodies will take care of us in the future. Pain works much in the same. We do not confront the aches and discomfort in our lives, so we run from it instead of embracing everything and leveraging it to your advantage. Seek pain out and transfer it into a different form of energy that can be distributed throughout. Everyday stressors are going to try and attack us and our mind, body, and soul every single day. It is incredibly vital to stay vigilant and open about giving yourself into the pain to have it become sort of a happy memory manifested into growth. When you take the pain and turn it into joy, you begin to turn negative into positive, bad situations into opportunities, it isn't positive thinking, but it has a positive mind frame from experience through the level of respect in negative acknowledgment.

As I started writing this very paragraph, my head was hurting quite a bit. As I awoke an extremely sharp pain, hit my frontal lobe, and I instantly felt it. So I got up and drank 16 oz. of room temperature water, made me some coffee, then proceeded to listen to meditation sounds with some binaural therapy to help ease the tension I was feeling. As I did this, it began to ease my mind slowly but more importantly, instead of popping two ibuprofen, which I usually would have done, I chose to sit and explore my pain. Really becoming mindful of my surroundings as well as my body and its aches.

As I explored, I listened with acceptance instead of demanding so much of it. Emotion and physical sensations are the human body's way of communicating with us. So I began to listen. After I took my immersion shower, the power of my cortisol was able to overshadow the headache and got me awake and ready to go. My mind felt sharp, and I felt as though I was prepared for the day again. Just remember the energy that is around you as well as inside of you. It is essential to know your body and be able to pay attention to anything that may feel off or odd or funny deep down in the pit of your stomach.

Here are some tips I've come up with that I personally practice when it comes to putting my energy back into alignment and refocusing it elsewhere:

- Meditation can be done in a variety of ways, but I feel people don't understand it, and so they don't feel the need for the use of it nor do they ever feel benefited afterward, and to those people I say, I totally agree. The first few times I didn't feel much maybe a little relief, but it did take time and much practice before I finally was able to figure out just how deep I was ready to go with it. There's passive mediation which is like a flow state in which you get so lost in the present moment you get completely sucked into it and begin to forget what is going in but instead get into this zone of productivity. Have you ever noticed that when you are on a roll you are thinking less, but things are clicking more? Boom! Also, there is applied and guided meditation in which you actually are taking the time to sit down and listen to a guide or some music and can just sit there and get to the same state but in a more concentrated mode.

- Eat some fruit or make a smoothie. In part, our gut really does play a huge role and so does the break down in chemicals of food with our brain chemistry so try eating something natural and good for you like some fruit or a good salad and see if you feel any different after making this transition. The more fructose or sugar and carbs something has, typically means it will have more of a negative effect. Of course, not all carbs are bad carbs, but the ways our bodies digest the carbs usually does it in the same ways it does sugars goes directly into the bloodstream and sends out glucose in massive amounts throughout the cells in your body until they are stuffed so much the excess gets stored into fat. That doesn't even sound like it would make us feel good.

- Working out and exercise are fantastic ways to redirect and improve your state of energy. Once you pivot all of that negative energy, it can feel very calming and therapeutic. In addition to you getting shredded and in shape which is never a bad thing. Make sure you are sweating, sweating releases toxins from the body as well as increasing more of a euphoric feeling and is boosting your heart rate which is ultimately burning that very same fat you put on with the food.

- Have you said hi to anyone? Have you talked to anyone today? Relationships are a massive part in the fulfillment of being human so we need to communicate with people in some way or starting the days off so lonely may decrease our energy levels also.

- Have you done what you love today? Have you invoked your passion and integrated it into your daily life. This is what will ultimately become your purpose in life so figure out if you partook in the love that lights the fire within you because if you have not then, of course, your energy is out of whack. Start focusing and not making excuses for being you and begin to love yourself enough to take the step in getting lost in a passion. It isn't wrong and in the year of 2019 more people will be doing or attempting to do businesses out of what they love anyway, so why are you any less capable? I've got news for you, you're not! You are more than capable of providing for your family. You are more intelligent than what people care to believe, and you are much more capable than even you feel. Start to take care of the life around you by first making sure you're okay and being able to go into any situations with clarity and belief knowing you can always be the one to solve the problem. Confidence will be your best friend.

When your negatives have been respected and acknowledged, they give you more power to overcome them. More willingness to take on the challenge, and instead of fighting the pain, you then start to accept the challenge and view it as such naturally. So pain thus turns into a craving and then you become unstoppable. With a growth mindset, nothing is too far from achievable, and no amount of obstacles are possible anymore, because then everything is observed as a way to level up from where you currently stand. The thing that took me so long to realize was that nobody was going to learn any of this for me. Nobody I knew was ever going through similar issues, and so I had to develop a system for myself to train these different levels of thinking. It's been harrowing. What sets me apart, however, is my willingness and ambition to overcome anything in the way of my goals.

P.O.A

"I've missed more than 9,000 shots in my career. I've lost almost 300 games. Twenty-six times I've been trusted to take the game winning shot and missed. I've failed over and over and over again in my life. And that is why I succeed."
- Michael Jordan

What is your P.O.A (Plan of Attack)? This needs to be meticulously planned, and that's the hardest part about it because right now as I'm sure you've noticed, you still only have very few pieces. This is where you begin to experiment with different ideas you've had or thoughts you've wanted to share. You have to start really putting yourself out there and see how far you go. Famous basketball superstar Michael Jordan said it best.

If you don't give yourself the freedom of often failing early on, you will always be fearful of the next move. The more you do. The more pieces to your vision of success you find. The more you can put the puzzle together as you go along. The goal is to enjoy putting the problem together. Not to rush it, and to always know that the more passion and heart you put in on it, the more beautiful the entire thing will look and it will give you something to feel proud of. Not make you feel as though it is a chore even to put it together. You've got to be able to remain optimistic and stand guard if the negativity that the world will show. This is why most people stop searching for the pieces. The universe has a way of testing and sifting out who really wants what they say they want. It isn't enough just to speak it into existence. You've actually got to put forth the work to obtain more of the vital pieces you need to move forward and keep progressing to build that momentum further and further.

Here's a better way to describe it, the puzzle play. Imagine that you have a new puzzle in front of you. With maybe two or three pieces from what you've read in the book plus your own pieces. These pieces represent experiences. Keep in mind the picture that this is going to describe is your entire life journey all the way to your version of success. So you fit these pieces together and find out where they go. Now that you've done that you keep attempting things in life and you find another part. Then next time maybe you don't, but the trick is always to keep striving for more pieces to make this the best picture you ever dreamed of. See, if you have a clear vision, that's why people get lost. If you don't even know what the picture looks like how do you know where to put the pieces and how the puzzle is supposed to look at the end? You can't, and it wastes more time and more energy. Do the correct 20% which is envisioning, engaging, and experimenting. The picture will become, and once it is solved, it will multiply and become a reality for you to live in.

This is a prime example also of why to treat failure with enthusiasm and create more opportunity for ourselves because what if you just missed a puzzle piece? Then it may take years before you can travel that level again and regain that lost puzzle piece. Everything in life is not guaranteed, but it is set. It will give you precisely what you ask of it, just not necessarily in the way you intended. It's as if the universe is the magic genie from Aladdin, and you must be careful or your wish. You must also be wary of what you ask of the world. If you want diamonds and that fancy lifestyle do not ask then why your life is so difficult. Audit to yourself what you are asking of the universe because the more you want, the harder these levels get and become. If you can muster up a growth mindset, you will see this can always be treated as a challenge or obstacle to overcome.

Start planning your plan of attack. Even if it's just to smile more. Try it out and try smiling in the mirror. Actually, practice smiling. There is nothing wrong with trying out new things like that. Start researching things that interest you and find that spark that you need to feel inspired. There's so much at our disposal with the technology we have to learn to embrace and not avoid. Have an open mind and start to look for those puzzle pieces of momentum keep pulling you forward!

Morning Routines and Hour Blocks

Part of being disciplined is being able to love yourself enough to begin your days correctly. Yes, precisely. There is actually a correct and incorrect way to go about your days, and it starts with your morning. Most people believe in the wrong way and stand by it as well, firmly. In no way, however, does correct mean one. Let me reiterate, in NO WAY does right mean ONE WAY. There are multiple avenues in which to go about a tailored morning, and this can lead to an even more productive day. Many different types of stressors can affect and alter us daily, which is why it is crucial to be able to get ahead and become vigilant early on. To do this, first, you must look and analyze your current morning routine. What does it consist of? Eating? Sleeping in? A workout? Journal? Well, all of these can be good, but there is a method to the madness.

Wake Up and Make a Choice, Then Drink Water

When we wake, often times we go into default where we are sort of tired or are dreading to muster up the strength to lift ourselves up out of bed. Then after we've snoozed a few times we're rushing to get out the door. This is mostly because of something you are not giving yourself time to do before all of this even happens. Before you also have the thought of not wanting to get up. When we wake up, we need to make a choice. It needs to become instinctual to the point you believe it so much it evolves into a lifestyle for you, and that is happiness.

Many people still have yet to figure out that happiness is a choice. The happiest people are not so because they have defaulted into joy, it is because they know how to combat negative and make that subconscious choice to be grateful for what they have. When you can genuinely become thankful for what you have, where you are and be at peace with your journey being the foundation, you break ground on your new abundant life. A luxurious experience is when you realize what is genuinely enriching to what you need and isolating that which your base needs are met.

Everybody's influences are either mainstream media, environment (negative news can be a part of this), or social media/circle. We are taught what to want. So why can we not teach ourselves more? Why do we idle in indulgence and settle with greed? Why is it that we do not get trained to become more? It's because nobody ever taught us also how to attack any of these issues or any of the things we go through. Even when it is things out of our control. Make the conscious decision every morning first thing to say to yourself, "I choose to be happy no matter what." This will trigger a response in the brain that is predetermined based on your perception now. So because you formed that belief, now it is so. Our minds are comprised of around roughly 80% water so by the time you've woken up your brain has lost a significant about of amount of it along with your body from all of the sweat from the night or maybe you had to use the restroom. So it is crucial for the first thing to be replenishing your intake and rehydrate the brain to begin the day. Try this out as long as you can bear and if you need to, log your results and see how you feel.

Write Your Thoughts

It is important to open yourself up and not be too crowded in your head. To do this, you can begin to write your thoughts. Also, you can write what you are grateful for each day as well. This helps instill a level of consistency for you. Write everything from thoughts to ideas, goals, dreams, and desires, the sky's the limit. Just write and express your feelings so that way, you can begin to clear your mind. A clear mind is a transparent life, which means you make clear decisions. Food, influences, and media can also affect your clarity, so this is why it's at least relevant to have things recorded down so that way you have a frame of reference for those ultra-creative moments where you just need to, and those days where you really just are not feeling it.

Pick a task

Whether it's writing or doing a workout, it is imperative to always finish something with some sort of progress. You can finish folding the clothes from the day before, or perhaps finish writing a chapter of that book you were going to start. Or even read 30 pages of a book before work. Whatever it is just remember that the idea of progression will build momentum throughout the day.

For me, I have no idea why but it was dishes. Dishes would always be an issue. How four people could use up so much, I could not tell you, but all I knew was it had been a pain to have always to come home and then wash everything so that it was clean for dinner. So I would hand wash as much as I could while my coffee would brew, that way it was clean all day, and it left me feeling great! Especially after work. So if you can drink water, write your thoughts, workout, finish a task and prime, then head to work well that is going to allow for one productive day.

Prime

Priming is important. This means in the morning after you have done all of that, you need to prepare yourself for the most beautiful day possible adequately. For example, let's say you've done all of the above, the next step then should be to close your eyes (if you need to) and think about today. Not tomorrow, not next week but today. Now visualize what will happen and literally play out the events that are supposed to take place as they happen. Truly see them, even the things that could go wrong, think about what today is supposed to consist of and tell yourself you will overcome any obstacles that are laid in front of you. Once you are primed (you will know) you can begin your day with anxiousness, preparation, and optimism. You are also more prepared for potential opportunities that may arise. Whenever we are closed off, we won't notice opportunity we will turn a blind eye to the thing we otherwise should be doing. This avoidance tactic is not necessarily one that we know we're doing because if we're around people of the same standard, then they will encourage the blind eye. You need to open up your eye. The priming will help you carry out the execution in all of the above. You will feel more prepared throughout the day when challenges do meet you at the forefront.

Workout

If you can or have enough time, even would like to substitute one of the above for this please get some exercise in. This is extremely vital! Some people do have very active jobs, and if this is the case, a light workout or intense workout after will suffice. For those that do not get as much exercise if you can at least finish one quick, intense workout, this will jolt your mind and body into action. Your neurons will fire releasing oxytocin through to the brain and causing a rise in serotonin and induces a sense of calm and happiness. This can allow your day to feel like it's already yours before it has even begun.

You do not need a gym or fancy equipment either. There are plenty of calisthenics workouts to help strengthen your body. The more you can also shift around your own body weight, the better. This will make it easier even to stretch, and it will help balance insulin levels so things will start to pick up a little and your body will almost feel as though it has awoken after years of hibernation. All of the above can help for a rewarding morning and transition into a very optimistic and productive day full of opportunity.

When you sleep in there is no time to think about what needs to be done. So your mental state is in constant scatterbrain all day because you failed to properly prime it to get ready for everything that is to come. It is at this moment that you need to realize how you can even prepare for the preparation.

First and Last

The first hour and the last hour are critical in the day. If you can control those parts of your day filled with routine. The in-between parts will seem much less overwhelming and intimidating. They will look much more comfortable in tackling the small problems and executing quicker for a more long-term approach. It is always about the bigger picture with the micro selections that are done thoroughly and correctly that can provide that sense of control, and that sense also includes ownership. Which, in turn, gives fulfillment. In the morning, make the above suggestions and in the evenings after all of the chaos that is life, just take a moment to breathe.

Unwind your mind and relax your brain, think about tomorrow and reflect on today, followed by maybe a book to read until you fall asleep. The next day you will be ready for whatever is to come and will have all of the steps necessary to take on any morning in the future regardless of what is going on outside and externally.

Harmony is the glue for everything. So you must be able to push past any pain or unwavering circumstance you may encounter because this is the threshold in which you grow. Working out is always the best analogy because when you lift weights, the goal is to make tiny micro-tears in your muscle fibers so that they can get bigger. However, this isn't where they grow. It is through adequate rest that these new muscles begin to form.

The same idea works for your brain. The more you work out your mind, the more you need proper rest for it to grow and you to become smarter and apply the knowledge you learn. You've got to learn to be as quiet in your mind as possible. The world is noisy and will continue to be so, but the use of shutting out the chatter will improve your productivity and ambition tenfold. Learn these tips for your morning, and it will slowly become more natural.

Always remember the morning will start the momentum for the entire day so make sure you begin it with the right mindset, the correct preparation and focus in the areas needed otherwise you may start to obtain bad habits and not realize until you are ten years down the line when you are wondering why nothing has changed. So many people fail to audit their life honestly. They feel they need to put on some sort of front like everything is fine and then 50 years go by, and they are in the same spot not even aware of the fact that their life could have had a dramatic impact on society. You just never know what you're perspective can do for someone, and people get so caught up in what everyone else thinks that they don't even feel the need to share it. It is hard to build yourself up, especially in the morning. That's why these next few chapters will be absolutely vital to read! They are going to talk about how to apply everything learned so far and how to actually implement it. This is where the action really starts happening because you are no longer held back by unknown feelings and thoughts. You now have a first level foundation to set up the work provided to sustain the happiness within yourself.

Jericho began stage two with a new motivation, to enjoy every step and to actually take in the beauty of it all. He also gained a new level of clarity by getting lost in the present with the end in mind. With the desire to just finish. Finishing first isn't so much on his mind anymore. It's as though he's more disciplined, especially after overcoming all of the upfront doubt that began to slowly pick away at his confidence and ability to believe he could continue on. Other runners stopped but not Jericho. There was a point where he had to go up a steep and treacherous hill he wasn't sure he'd be able to get up, but he prevailed taking him to the second checkpoint.

Once he arrived, it was there that he noticed he had pain in his foot. The medical team quickly examined it and proceeded to explain that his feet began to swell due to the heat and so that gave him blisters that have now become infected. He listened to instructions thoroughly and started the recovery process with a hopefulness that he could continue on despite the fear building inside of him. First, the bladder and now this, but he pressed on with the notion that you may get infected, but you always have to be willing to get your feet wet to get through to the end. Once bandaged up and rested, he began into the third stage with not only more overall gratitude and momentum, but some profound courage as well to carry out his new plan of attack and to keep taking steps to enjoy the beauty that lies within all of this hardship. Just as he had to as a child.

Part III: Spiritual Health & Energy

Stage Three: The Atacamenos Trail

Jericho so far has had a new mindset shift, he's been able to open up his perspective quite a bit to different ideas of what this race is truly about. He has also taken so much accountability for the things he hasn't been able to control so far, such as not having water the first leg of the infection during the second. He's formed a deep level of gratitude during all of that as well. He feels incredibly entranced in the fact that he's still able to push forward. Typically if an infection is bad enough, they do not necessarily let you go on.

That was his reinforcement that he isn't done! He was able to concentrate on the present and create a new level of focus to create clarity, which gave him more momentum into this new phase of being in spirit. With all of that, the amount of discipline he's had to endure within the mind has also allowed him to formulate what success means to him and create his new plan of attack which is now to enjoy every step instead of focusing on how much further he had to go. This has now allowed him to become more aware of his energy and will grant him the ability to raise his frequency to help aid him through the Atacamenos Trail.

Energy for the World

"Don't get set into one form, adapt it and build your own, and let it grow, be like water"
-Bruce Lee

When I first began this journey of self-discovery, one thing I had never taken into account was why I had always not made confident choices? Why was I repeatedly making the same mistakes over and over? It took a while before finally coming to some sort of explanation other than pragmatism. What it came down to was not coming to terms and being honest with myself, and actually being an adult and gaining accountability towards the things I usually ran from. I would participate in recurring actions that at the time, I knew would only further hinder my growth, as they definitely did. I would always talk to myself saying things like, "I know it may set me back, but I deserve this because I work hard." The instant gratification weighed more than the vision and took me out of my element.

This type of encounter would happen often, and in combination with the popularly known 'fake it till you make it' mentality, this can be a recipe for disaster. Maybe not now, but perhaps down the road. From what I've observed, typically it goes like this; People will do well for a while, then a hurdle or bump in the way will come, and it alters either their perception and/or their motivation. They deter from the path that was initially intended.

For example, most hip-hop artists love to write and perform music. Then they make tons of money and start buying cars and drugs and start getting caught up in that aspect. This is about the time when you hear of all of the controversies happen or other unforeseen circumstances. When you begin to derail from the origin of your intent you begin to experience avoidance because you are not dealing with every aspect of the issues inside of your realm, you're merely indulging in the byproduct of the work. This is when people become addicts or become mentally unstable.

That's why building the foundational aspect of this is so important because not everything will go right every time and if you can begin to take a calculated risk and not hold back, the seemingly grim and mundane future of repetitive routine can start to change into abundance and variety. All the while still employing patience and gratitude as well as living through passion, well then money or no money you've already won.

Surrender

To gain control you must surrender to the current. You do not fight water because of the amount of work it takes to overpower the force of the water is impossible. So what to do? Well as Chinese actor, director, martial artist, instructor and philosopher Bruce Lee stated,

"Empty your mind, be formless, shapeless, like water. Now you put water into a bottle, it becomes the cup; You put it in a teapot it becomes the teapot. Now water can flow or it can crash."

Embracing your circumstance does not mean accepting defeat or surrendering to the will of life. Not at all. Quite the opposite actually. By embracing your situation, you are releasing yourself from the irresponsibility and taking ownership. You are learning to become water. To flow. That means accountability is going to cause for more action than previously done before. Why? Progression and Diligence! Let's take a look and analyze;

You've taken accountability, and now you are owning every problem. Going with the flow of water and steering accordingly based on the current. The only other head-scratching thought is what now? You have no money, no idea, and no knowledge, where do you start?

Thousands of dollars in debt and no way to take care of your problem accept to live for today, get a drink and live substandard to low upper class just to get by enough to pay bills. No, now you isolate the issues and pay each according to either interest rate, or smallest to most significant. These are widely known as snowball and avalanche methods of paying off debt. Let's forget about money though, because it isn't about that and I'll tell you why. Money is a tool to get you the things you need to either help or hurt people. Either way, if all you do when you're broke is stress about bills, that's all you will do with money also. The only difference being more amounts to be responsible for. It just isn't sustainable and is not helping anyone except the entitled part of the ego trying to convince you that you're special and deserve special treatment from the world.

It is okay to feel special and feel that you are destined to greatness. You have that right as a human being entirely, but you cannot think that you are entitled to it. You are not even entitled to your next breath. You have to do the things that allow your body to keep functioning, but if you stop that work or nutrition and sleep, your body shuts down. There's nothing we are entitled to and the sooner you take hold of that concept, the easier it is to shift into the more embraced stage of this encounter.

Instead, what you need to do is focus on everything that has already been discussed in this book so far. It's designed to give you strength when you need it to make the decisions you wouldn't typically have found the confidence to create.

Once you've fully embraced your circumstance and the amount of control you don't have, that automatically gives you back all of that control. Now that you are honest to yourself about what is truly going on and that you need to be like water, you will now glide with the current and learn to adapt and use it to your advantage to get you to where it is that you need to go. Anticipate the shortcomings but strive for the stars.

Don't allow self-doubt to deter your confidence. Be yourself and never be ashamed of it. Then take the losses and gains and view failure as an opportunity. Now nothing can stop you! Embracing your problems and dealing with your issues, finally taking responsibility will now present to you a sense of pride within yourself, and soon you will notice all of the progression that begins to take place.

You'll wonder why you ever stopped yourself from growing before because who knows how far you could have been.

What is essential is not to dwell but to learn and push forward, continuing to become a lifelong learner. One thing that I always found so intriguing was the fact that life has such harmonious stability. You need some negatives to induce positive behavior, and positive to counteract too much negative. You need to put yourself out there but not care what people think. Viewing others but only compare objectively. Visualization and work ethic. In knowing this, just realize that life is a balancing act, so try not to get too excited in times of happiness and not too saddened in times of sorrow. Be at one with yourself. Calm your mind and soul to be at peace and in a middle flow state of being.

Vibration & Frequency

"As you think you vibrate. As you vibrate you attract."
Abraham Hicks

Energy is quite an amazing aspect that allows for much of the ideas in this book to come together. First, let's discuss what energy is.

Three Definitions of Energy:

- *The strength and vitality required for sustained physical or mental activity.*
- *Power derived from the utilization of physical or chemical resources, especially to provide light and heat or to work machines.*

- *The property of matter and radiation that is manifest as a capacity to perform work (such as causing motion or the interaction of molecules).*

There is way too much to learn about energy. Perhaps I can begin a journey and write a book on that as well, but the idea of human energy is when you involve auras and chakras and tap into your mind, body, and spirit. The other two are basically chemical energy and physical energy. Physical energy includes things that physically transfer different forms of energy in response to additional power. Much like a microwave heating your food, or us all having potential energy converted to kinetic energy when we move. When it comes to chemical energy, these are the burning of oil or photosynthesis. Plants take solar energy and convert it into chemical energy. They take the water, carbon dioxide, and the solar rays to produce compound and oxygen that we breathe and in turn breathe out more carbon dioxide for it. The world amazes me! I am nowhere near an expert on this stuff, but there is an underlying theme behind these common forms of energy.

If you notice, each one of these has the similarities of constant of work and sustained activity. It may be in different ways, but each of these forms works to complete and convert to ensure any given task. Which means bringing energy is work in itself, but there's the good news! It means that it's been within you all this time. You have the power to radiate. Energy can neither be created nor destroyed only transferred or converted. You only you have the power of using whatever is inside of you and transform it into kind, positive and compassionate energy that you can use to attract the same levels of energy not just outwards but inwards as well.

Remember that boss that always had that energy to keep going and pushing the boundaries, and while you found it rather annoying most times, the productivity levels were insurmountable? Exactly. You remember that boss. You remember the energy they brought to the work day every single morning. It's essential to provide useful energy every single day and bring that positive energy because not everyone can. Being a leader requires you to take the first step by putting in the work to sustain that positive outlook. Also to coincide with this, energy is moved to produce. So while power is working, it is also moving and transferring at all times, bouncing back and forth so to speak.

Knowing this is vital to realize that the energy in action you put out is what you get back. Let's take a look at the traffic example again; in traffic, you acknowledge your emotions and show them respect. Now you ask the three questions above, take a few deep breaths, and this will give you the power realign your energy. When you put out negative emotional energy, you get the same response because that's the only response you allow yourself to feel. This is why it's crucial to be able to have control over your emotions. Remember, they will want to drive, but they are not old enough, DO NOT LET THEM!

So what energy are you bringing to the table every day? Is it positive, upbeat, and motivational energy? Or sluggish, half-hearted, dysfunctional energy that breeds problems and limited views. Make sure you take a step back and sincerely ask yourself, 'What am I doing?' and 'How am I working toward what I want every day?' This is when you can begin to identify which type of mindset you have. There are growth and fixed mindsets, and everyone falls under one of these two categories.

Belief Systems

"Don't let fear or insecurity stop you from trying new things. Believe in yourself. Do what you love. And most importantly, be kind to others, even if you don't like them."
-Stacy London

Pragmatism began in the 1870s by philosophers William James, John Dewey, and Charles Sanders Peirce. They explored the notions that thoughts could be a tool for prediction, problem-solving, and action. This means trial and error. Not based off of our predetermined reality. This means using a practical application to figure out the best and more sensible way to go about things. Not theorizing but actualizing and taking action to whittle away at the not so practical approaches. When you do something, and it goes to complete shit, well then you know what is now feasible and what is not. It isn't based on theory anymore but is now solely predicated on the effects concocted from this experiment. Think of pragmatism as a way to adapt to an ever-changing world. To cope with the change, you must partake; otherwise, you become like Mr. Scrooge from A Christmas Carol and don't want any part of the changes so reject the practical aspects right off of the bat. This is an in-depth subject, so I do implore you to read over this paragraph a few times until you move on to the next. Let's go over a couple of definitions for both uses of the words.

Pragmatism -

- *(Philosophy) An approach that assesses the*

truth of the meaning of theories or beliefs in terms of the success of their practical application.

Pragmatic -

- *Dealing with things sensibly and realistically in a way that is based on practical rather than theoretical considerations.*

These are two definitions that mean the same thing when it comes to making decisions and dealing with anything. Be practical about the situations as opposed to playing out hypothetical scenarios or lies will help propel you to make the best decision moving forward. If you get caught up in knowing what is practical but refusing it, that's how most people end up in the same spot after so many years. It also goes back to self-love. Do you love yourself enough to see the pragmatic reasons as to why you are not furthering in life? Much as an addict of something, our brain doesn't sense practicality. It is instead skewed, and all you begin to see is the reality. Life sucks you need something to unwind, and you have the money. However last week you did the same thing, and you are in the same predicament as last week. Or you bought groceries and thought you did everything right but have no money left over to save. "What am I doing wrong?" you ask. Well, the answer is you are not being practical at all. See this is why auditing is vital because you take the little extra time to get into the habit of focusing your attention on what's working as opposed to what's not. Follow success and adversity. As you continue to develop these stories of what feels comfortable and familiar on repeat, the brain becomes more and more inclined to believe you based on the thought process you're going through. Remember your thoughts eventually dictate your habits, so oversee them. Stay disciplined in your focus.

Being pragmatic is not something most people are willing to face. When's the last time you did something because it was practical and not with an intent shifted to a particular focus? If your 5'3 chances are you will not be the first person of that height to be in the NBA. Practical. It isn't necessarily your fault. We have been programmed by so much, and influence plays a significant role in that. However, there are three different types of truths we all form to create our sense of belief and what is practical. How we rationalize our decisions can be based on predetermined factors that can be leveraged to your advantage.

The power of belief is real. It can truly make or break your limitations. The conviction stems from what you know to be accurate and not. Just as the environment plays a critical factor in how we perceive certain things. Much of belief also has to do with exposure, and that dives down deeper because what this can also do for you is allow a sense of validation that something will happen no matter what.

Truthfully do you believe that you will achieve great things in life yes or no? Now, why is or isn't that? You must be able to justify that you have something to offer this world because there's no survival without that confidence in yourself that you can take on any problem and have the capabilities to solve it. Belief can give motivation, and with that comes visualization because you can see it, feel it, taste it, and that is when you begin to believe it wholeheartedly.

That's why it's so vital to be able to become emotionally stable and have certain aspects of your foundation in place otherwise you may not be able to find the belief being caught up with so many internal and external distractions. Also, the process, upon beginning the formation of that belief in yourself, can start to become more natural in the self-awareness of who you are. What self-belief also does is create a form of self-love, because in turn, when we believe, then there is subsequently more clarity as to what kind of potential you have.

Self-doubt is what plagues us all daily. Think about a post you didn't share or that book you never wrote, or that chance you never took. The one thing they have in common? You doubted yourself before you even believed it was possible. Why though? Why do we continually sabotage our future selves by indulging into these mindless head games? Doubt comes from fear. You're scared so instead of trying and failing, you doubt and do not work. We talked about fear and what it can do to paralyze you and so this is the part where you need to jump. Everything familiar up to this point may be trying to tell you that it's the wrong move, but that's your mind's way of getting out of conformed life and into the life of acquisition.

We are designed to serve and survive. Why not have a purpose and live! There's no reason not to. Whether it's some old job that's got you down or just the norms of everyday weighing down on you because there is no light at the end of the tunnel. Let me tell you there may not be light now, but the more you go exploring, the quicker you will find it. It may take agonizing pain and time to move rocks and push boulders, but if you do, there will be abundance at the end. Even if the end of the tunnel is you getting through your day, as long as you have your belief in check nothing can really deter you from the path of execution and finishing what you set out to.

When you start to really develop this, you begin to make decisions, then based on discipline because you now know the repercussions of not doing things out of self-love. It creates self-doubt. So you do have self-love or self-doubt coursing through your veins? Either way just by knowing this information gives you such an advantage. Most people do not even get this far. What this will also do is it will allow pursuance in what you're strengths are and allow for a more sense of enjoyment and practicality.

Your Truth

"Follow the truth of the way. Reflect upon it. Make it your own. Live it. It will always sustain you." Gautama Buddha

There are three different types of truths to think about. There is self-meaning, which is your truth, so this is what you believe to be true in your heart. Religion, for example, would be your truth. Then there is a societal truth, one in which the people decide the fact such as what is in popular culture. Then lastly there is an absolute truth which is an objective truth. These are about things such that have been done by the scientific method that has been proven to be true. This truth holds a place in the world, such as all of the scientific laws, most of which are applied in everyday life, including with the writing of this book. So now we'll move onto each truth, and how to form them into one cohesive place you can explore and develop your own opinions without caring what anyone thinks.

Your Version of Truth -

- This is what you believe, and is formed by the external ideas and influence combined with intrinsic values and emotions all tied and wrapped together and coated by an outer shell that is exposure.

Societal Truth -

- This is what society believes to be accurate, and is formed by popularity or a majority belief to one idea or influence of culture.

Objective Truth -

- This is proven scientific facts and laws that always apply and can never be altered unless disproved through repeated proper experimentation. This has already been formed by the theorists, physicists, and other scientists in various fields that have already proven laws such as nature, motion, and gravity.

The ways that these all play a role into belief are as follows:

You begin to form a truth based on everything you are personally experiencing. Societal aspects of what is popular along with the people in your own environment telling you or swaying you in a particular direction will begin to add onto the preexisting truth. It alters. Then in combination with considering what is known to be right on merit and what has already been realized the belief can either progress or regress.

This is when people start to feel hopeless and resort to

the last options as a first priority. Do not get caught into a cycle of despair. This is why exposure is so crucial and why the saying goes, "you are who you hang out with." It isn't so much in a literal sense as it is in an abstract sense. It should read, "you are who you are exposed to most." That has, at least for me, always seemed a bit more accurate.

Apart from being practical is also knowing that happiness is not a second nature deal. It doesn't just happen; it takes patience, persistence, and poise. It takes massive belief and insane amounts of gratitude. It brings perspective, and also it takes discipline. Once you wake up and apply the ideas covered thus far the sooner you can realize how much work, and how much of choice happiness truly is. It is something that nobody can take away from you.

So many people reading right now will think about how many of their friends don't seem like they are trying very hard to be happy but more so trying hard to get everything they want such as new car and a new house and a new watch and the latest, fanciest phone. It isn't about that. The fact of the matter is they can have the lovely million dollar mansion if they want, but once that goes, what do they have? Money can be obtained. Time cannot. So don't waste it solely on the pursuit of money because you're actually losing more time on yourself in the process. It is much better to use the time and work on yourself to reap the benefits of sustainable wealth as opposed to a fortune that isn't being utilized correctly. Invest in yourself above all because that is where the real longevity lies. Which, in turn, is where legacy is created.

During the path, he came across one of the NASA stations where films use the terrain for specific film shoots or NASA themselves send out rovers for test runs on the Salt Flats. Jericho, however, was feeling extremely exhausted about three-quarters of the way through. He had spoken with a couple of people back at the last checkpoint about where they were from. One was from Australia and had been doing this for a few years now. The other had been volunteering a few years ago and decided to try it out For once and loved the idea of the journey and wanted to keep reliving it. Almost as if this very race was the pinnacle and to reach that point of bliss was virtually possible for it to trickle down into who they had become. The thrill kept them so alive throughout other areas that they kept coming back.

He all of a sudden, felt a jolt of inspiration and with it came a need to try and finish first again because he wanted that same level of experience under his belt. He knew with his infections, he needed to keep a good pace. All that kept running through his mind was everyone in front of him and memories of his checkered past. Of failing and never having anything, and that boosted his ego back into primal mode. After the extraordinary moment of frustration he concludes he's earned the gratitude and momentum but now to continue that instead of getting upset, he needs to harness that and release a new vibration to keep the fire spreading. Not only that but the next checkpoint is a rest day and so not only will Jericho rest but he will also get a chance to strengthen his newfound conclusions so far and can allow him to re-center and regain the control he felt he may be losing. As he is slowly unraveling the gifts, he stumbles through the third checkpoint, and he instantly

dropped and began resting with some water at his side.

As he awoke, he now knew what was getting him by and keeping him out of his own head and seeing things objectively. His new energy level had now granted him the awareness of empathy and the relationships that have been built thus far. By speaking through their own experiences, it began normalizing things for the first timers and allowing for laughter in the face of fear, inflictions and even worse, the idea that it's every person for themselves. It made him personally feel as if he were not alone and had been going through much of the same egotistical and self-worth battles of comparison they had also been experiencing.

Part IV: Relationships & Empathy

Stage Four: The Salt Flats

Upon entering the salt flats, Jericho had a chance at a full days rest. Before the last few legs of the marathon, they allow for a full day because this will be the biggest haul of effort yet. The night before, while Jericho couldn't sleep, he gathered around the other runners nearby and joined a conversation about winning. One of the runners had mentioned that he was coming to the race to win but could not lie about the fact that his perspective of that changed after the first portion. Others put in their two sense as well and so Jericho felt like the only one feeling as though this was impossible. He spoke up and explained that he kept wanting to create this idea in his head that he could win.

Then it diminished as he went on when he knew the acknowledgment of getting first or the amount of attention it would give him would never happen. In turn, he doubted everything just like his existence as a kid and almost didn't even get to this point. Then he went on to say that it was really being grateful for each moment, each hardship that made it all worth it and made him realize that he needs to be happy with every step. Not every win.

The others truly accepted him and his emotions, making him feel like he was a part of a much bigger family. Ones that supported him and were willing to listen felt beyond ready to finish this race. He thought he had learned all that was needed to know about being grateful, using the momentum had already begun to create and the new positive energy he had going in. He felt he was ready, and the new friends he had made along the way made it more than confident. Now it's a team effort, and maybe that's just the push he needed.

The salt flats were entering the most challenging part of the entire race. They are an uneven, running shoe chewing moon rock terrain that can bring even the most seasoned runners to a slow walk. Covered with hard-packed salt sheets, razor-sharp crystals growing out of the ground and frozen cauliflower heads that can crumble into a hole taking your foot with it. This was going to be the ultimate test.

The final application of everything he had ever learned all put into action. He was more fearful now than he had ever been, but knew that he needed to throw the infliction upon himself aside, along with any comparison with others. He needed to keep his level of

ego at a harmonized level so that his expectations would not become falsified to the point where he would make excuses. He was well aware of what he has gained this far. Would it be enough, though?

Empathy for Others

"Nobody cares how much you know until they know how much you care." – Theodore Roosevelt

A A Psychologist by the name of Giacomo Rizzolatti M.D. was the first one to identify mirrored neurons. These are actual cells in the brain that mimic the things we see. The first experiments were done in the 1980s when he tested the response of macaque monkeys. He quickly noticed certain parts of the brain (the same elements that can be found carefully related to humans) firing whenever they would reach for a peanut or take a bite at it. Then the person performing the experiment would contact for the peanut to hand it to the monkey, and the same neurons would fire. This literally means that equal parts of the brain would fire when the person would give them a peanut, and when the monkey would reach for the peanut. Since then, extensive research has been done to map the imaging of the brain in humans during this very process, and it has been carefully compared.

The problem with getting the same study done with humans is it requires direct electrodes to the brain, so imaging is all we have when it comes to that. The main difference as far as what that means is with the monkey it starts to be able to be pinpointed down to the exact individual neuron whereas with humans it comes down to a three-millimeter outline for which could lie the answer. It is proven that the premotor cortex is what is the underlying part of the brain that is most affected by this, which does suggest that it is a mirrored effect on those specific cells in your mind.

In conclusion, though this is why realizing who you hang around with and what you are exposed to is so important. Everything we see is likely to be imitated on some level. This is why peer pressure is so real. Those parts of your brain plus your emotional need for connection means, of course, you will do that which you know you shouldn't. Why? Well because everyone else is doing it.

So next time someone says, "If they go jump off a bridge are you going to"? You say I actually might depending on how many people are doing it and what kind of response it triggers in my premotor cortex. They'll look at you like you're insane. I'm just kidding do not tell them that but just know that those are where sayings like that sort of come from. From the notion that we do tend to match the actions of those around us. So make sure you are surrounding yourself with the right people; otherwise, you could be headed more quickly to a place or in a situation in which you do not want to be.

It always starts with the mind so the sooner we can figure this brain of ours out and why we are the way we are we can better understand how to change ourselves each day for more and more progression. The key is to progress all the time. To continually be getting better and better until you feel there is no more left to learn (which actually is impossible by the way). You can try, but from my personal experience, the more you learn, the more you realize you don't know. For me, this is encouraging, and so you should begin your journey as soon as possible and do not hold back any longer. Take what you have learned so far and reread any parts that may seem fuzzy.

Remember this book is to act as your own reference guide. To learn these chapters and become fluent. These will all come into play in your life is some form or another. The sooner you can follow these or put your own spin on it, the faster you will be propelled to fulfillment. I am in no way guaranteeing you millions of dollars, but if you work, you will gain fulfillment and abundance in your life, and others have had better income become a byproduct of that real transformation. It is all just a matter of how much you're willing to let go of, and how much with how long you're ready to sacrifice for.

Have you honestly thought about the things you've given up? Was it enough? Did you do all that you could today? Did you muster up the strength to combat that negative energy and harness it into productive energy? These are the things you've got to integrate into your psyche. Remember, we are our thoughts. So allow clarity into your mind to bring clarity into your life and into your heart.

Relationships are often overlooked as much as bad as that sounds. This piece of the pillar system is quite substantial. Remember the last time you thought the popular kid had all the opportunity and all of the luck. It seemed very unfair simply because from the outside looking in it was portrayed as though they didn't do well in school yet were still able to accomplish more than you were.

Well, this has very much to do with the types of networking and relationships they built based on the school setting. See, nowadays the school system, as well as the entire world, is all social media based. Before, maybe about 10 years ago or so, this was already happening with kids on a smaller scale. Instead of globally, it was locally through individual schools but was mostly all encompassed internally. Now so in this day and age, it is not the case. Influence is everywhere, and as that powerful influence has pointed out before it is not always the best decision maker.

It is always essential to take into account that saying, "you are the top three to five people you associate yourself with." The people you are around have everything to do with where you are, but I also believe exposure and environment play a role here as well. We will go over those in later chapters but as for the friend aspect, audit who it is you spend your time around and briefly compare similarities and differences in your lives. If you can see more than a few in either direction, the results become more explicit. This is when the time comes to focus on who it is you are, and if you need to take a step back to figure out what it is, that makes you tick. Most people will try and tell you they're doubts and fears based on their own perception, but if this is the case, you may not need them in your life anyway.

You do not need small weight, we are heavy as it is. So free yourself as best you can. The lighter you become, the lighter you feel. Learn to strip the weights that are not benefiting you. In the fitness and weight lifting industry, you have to do more reps with a smaller load, and you will eventually grow somewhat, but you will mostly increase limited strength. Whereas pushing the resistance and upping the weight will give you growth and strength. You've got to level up the weight if you want to level up in life. An easy way to a plateau is to stay with the same routine and pressures.

Change things up and keep yourself guessing. The more people you connect with, the deeper your significance in life feels as a whole. Social interaction is an extremely effective way to combat anxiety and depression. Given that you can communicate, most often than not, these real friends, spouses, or partners are the ones that are there to make sure you are staying the course. They will notice things wrong with you before you will know you are showing it. Some are incredibly good at faking it, but typically it will show through behavior. The ones that find it is particularly hard are the secluded ones. Where you disconnect with everyone and feel as though nobody cares. When you notice that it is only due to lack of communication and your unwillingness to figure out how to verbalize these emotions. If you truly have no one or feel you have no one, try starting a social media account right now and do not post at all. Just engage and find people with similar interest and begin to form friendships. Media and other outlets spew out stats on why social media is a detriment to our society when it's able to reach people from all parts of the globe and interconnect like-minded people for these very scenarios.

The problem lies in the inability to engage effectively. Most people simply like pictures and comment some trash talk because someone has it better than them. Instead of picking people up and genuinely relating to another human being. Stay inside of your real persona and be yourself because people tend to lose who they are once they start posting. Just stay humble and stay the course, but try to make friends because we are a naturally social being, so it's in our biology to interact and seek to be understood.

This also goes the same for romantic relationships as well. Do not meddle unless you are serious and also in addition to this, allow yourself to be with someone that is both going to push you to grow and also has the potential to grow with you simultaneously. It is essential to realize that increasing and separately doing so, is entirely different when being compared to growing together. Even in just knowing that can make all of the difference. The idea of communication is crucial, so if you have not yet had friends or have established connections with people, I wouldn't even recommend getting into a relationship at all. People with a lack of these connections tend to get overwhelmed by all of the emotions that are triggered by having a whole other human and their feelings as well.

It can be a lot to bear at one time for some, and what happens if this is the case is those people feel as though something is wrong, and begins to act distant, not as consistent when it comes to things like their daily mood. It will fluctuate, and it will seem as though you are kind of trapped after a while, which in turn can lead to breakups, divorce, domestic violence, infidelity, all stemming from you unwilling to communicate your feelings into actual words. I realize this can be difficult, but that is why it's always best to practice because we all get better with it when we consciously practice this.

Even taking communication a step further, if you're ordering from a drive-thru, how thorough are you with that order? Very! Because you know how many times the miscommunication leads to a wrong burger, or missing fries again. It is so vital to be clear and concise with the ways we feel but not get too emotionally involved so we can keep the most grounded mind possible. We will discuss emotions in depth later, but for now, just know to be mindful of your feelings but do not let them drive the communication part of it. Instead, feel what you feel and express it in a way that is both practical and will allow the other person to feel like you are talking to them and not at them. Just genuinely be willing to be vulnerable. That is what a relationship is, and ultimately, what love is. To accept the vulnerabilities within ourselves as well as others. So talk about feelings do not let them take the wheel. You can talk about the kids and to the kids while they're in the back seat. Emotions are like children in the back seat. If you want a more quiet and composed ride, you just may have to acknowledge your feelings a bit more.

So keep the relationships that you have with everyone in your life secure, concise, and to the point. What I've found is that many people waste time on things that don't matter so also figure out what matters to you during this process. People will love fitness for two weeks and then jump typically to nursing or simply cannot stop discussing gossip and drama. Later next month into scuba diving and the following month they are so impacted and become a vegan. How many people do you know like this? Just so unsure of what the next move is. Well, it isn't scuba diving. Unless you genuinely love scuba diving then go for what you love!

The problem most people have is this switching, going back and forth with figuring out what you like to do. Then on top of that have to have a job, so now it's almost as if your time will be taken up by work, children(if you have them), Netflix, going to the grocery store, cooking dinner, then bed. So build more relationships with people like-minded and that encourage what you're doing. It's okay to go back and forth but really do it with an intent of finding that one thing. What is truly important is that you are open and allow people to help you with ideas or just inspiration in general. The more genuine the relationship, the better you can become surrounded by the right people.

The Gift of Presence

"You build on failure. You use it as a stepping stone. Close the door on the past. You don't try to forget the mistakes, but you don't dwell on it. You don't let it have any of your energy, or any of your time, or any of your space." - Johnny Cash

When we laugh, we give ourselves the luxury of letting go. At that moment we are not thinking because we are in the present moment. The power of this presence can heal, and it can be used to lift as well as open up potential. Think back to a time you were really upset, and somebody did something funny, or you saw something that made you laugh. You may have gotten sad again right after, but at that moment you found the goodness within the present moment enough to actually let out a very expressional form of happiness.

An excellent way to get better at this is practice. Yes, practice. It may sound odd, but I was, and I believe most of us unconsciously were, hardwired to take life extremely seriously. When I couldn't let go, I became wound so tight I snapped, which showed through reactive actions such as playing the victim or allowing my emotions to override me. This happened often, and I would get set off so easily. Surely you have experienced going off because someone yelled at you or getting upset because somebody criticizes you but little do we know it is about something much more significant than just that in itself.

In feelings of frustration and irritability, we may not handle it as well as we could if we were just able to take that mini-vacation in mind for one small second, at least enough to feel grateful for the contrast, which is the reality. What I have always found truly interesting is our ability to laugh at ourselves. I think once we begin to become too hard on ourselves, that is what can lead to judgment or resentment, not in just us, but others based on the situation that's causing the tension. I have always said life is cunning so we may as well be able to laugh at it.

It is okay to smile, even in the face of adversity. It shows how far you have come, and if you begin to take the time to smile simply, you will start to see that the hard times don't seem as prolonged. They go by more quickly, and this speeds up any lulls or productivity issues because you can push forward and that starts to form new habits. It trains the mind to become more at ease with the things that are out of our control. We often times try to control every outcome, which leads to disappointment and false expectation and eventually becomes devastating to the untrained ego. Whereas if we were just to be present, there would be no worry of past or future, only the now which could potentially allow us to accomplish so much more than we think.

Many people are not consciously aware of what goes on in their mind, let alone the things that go on around them. They believe that they are somewhat entitled to things in this world, and that couldn't be further from the truth. The world does not owe you anything. There is negative around you, there will be naysayers, and there will be self-doubt. You will not want to keep going, but if it's what you love, then you will. You will keep pulling yourself forward and will not accept defeat regardless of the odds. It is at this moment you can be okay, and you can slowly ease into complete mindfulness. Not worrying about things that may happen, but instead just being in the present moment enjoying what life has to offer you now.

Too many times, we forget where we are. We know we are unhappy, but we do not explore any other emotions aside from the euphoric ones such as sadness or our anxiety. Why are we so quick to examine and identify with these as opposed to happiness and excitement? It is because we feel the shame of having these instead of taking responsibility for ourselves and our decisions, so we become too harsh and attack the wrong reason. This causes an imbalance and now throws us off our game. We need to embrace every piece of the puzzle because life is like an unsolved puzzle. So this means when you get angry to explore that emotion. Why are you mad? Is it benefiting you to be angry? Will it change anything to remain angry? What is it that is causing my anger? Am I anxious or unprepared for something? All the while, in knowing how to become familiar with these, you can also begin being aware of where you are and be entirely in the present.

When you do things like meditation, this activates the same power. Most think that meditation is this idea where your mind is entirely blank when really it is the opposite. In giving your control up, you gain full control. The same way it works with the current of life. You can let your thoughts run free, but they do come back, and the less you stir from their outcries as you do not pay them any emotion the more they conform to your new levels of focus. It is a compelling way to not only start the day but to always be able to take a second for yourself to recoup and recharge your battery.

The misconstrued opinion on mindfulness is that it is all about positivity when, in reality, that is not it at all. It is about being aware. Being completely aware of your body, your emotions, and your thoughts. While being present enough to be immersed into the moment enough to not feel pain not feel pleasure but instead just feel. Not attach any sort of story to it of happy or sad, but just feel. See, hear, smell, and experience it all as it unfolds. It has nothing to do with positivity but instead totally at peace with everything. It is quite an incredible power when you can use it. Not being a total jerk and ignoring people either, most won't understand why you are acting so high and mighty, but with this, you can just apologize for it coming off that way. You do not need to explain yourself. This is something you will struggle with. You do not need to explain yourself though because most will not have enough context to encourage but will have limited background enough to judge. Nobody has time for approvals you've just got to get working on yourself.

Some studies show our mind wanders up to 47% of the time. That means for a little under half the time we are not present at the moment with people because we have already left into moments of the past or future. So train your mind into being in the now. What you practice grows stronger. You can, with repetition, reshape your brain into becoming better at being in the present.

You have to also be open in your mind because you have to be ready not to judge yourself or get mad if your thoughts do wander around. You just calmly bring it back to the place you are in and refocus on your breaths and be aware of you and your body. Mindfulness can lower your cortisol levels and stress too so it can, in turn, help allow for more clarity into your life and your goals. Shame can rob your brain of change and will not let this growth happen, so be kind and always be kind to yourself. You still have the power to transform. To become what you want to be. It's going to take hard work and much practice, but you will feel better the more consistent you are with it.

Remember this takes time. One key thing you can do to speed this up is get lost. Get lost in things that make you forget about the world. Start there. Do what your passion is and realize that if it is money you're after, that will come later. People don't seem to understand that money is a tool, and it can also become a byproduct for that passion and purpose as well. That's why you're able to use it as a tool now and can continue all the way up the ladder.

See it isn't money you're after. It's something else. Whether that is a work-life balance, a nice car, or even if it is money, well you do need money to enhance that ability. However, if your intent is just to get more money that will not be sufficient for very long and those people will see very soon why. The fact of the matter is everyone wants money to do things. When in reality, all it takes is money to do things. Save up, work, build, get strategic, and play off of your past failures. That's the secret.

Money is also an amplifier. That's why I'm putting this in here is because I want you to know that money does have an essential role in success but only when you have the right mindset. It will not stay in the hands of the foolish long, doesn't do well with morals. It doesn't have any worth other than transactional value. It encourages you to spend it because it's there. So will you have self-love and self-discipline or will you indulge and be broke again very soon. It all depends on how you become before you gain any financial success or wealth. If there is also anyone that builds financial success or wealth, those things will come as soon as you implement the critical components needed to create it. The universe always knows when you're ready so that's why you've got to remain actively patient and invest in yourself as early on as you can.

Expose Yourself

J.k Rowling, the author of the 'Harry Potter' books, was on government assistance in 1994 when she had gotten a divorce and was barely able to feed her daughter. Three years later, when she wrote the first Harry Potter book, she manually typed out 90,000 words each time it got sent out to a new publisher because she couldn't afford a computer to photocopy the pages. Finally, a small publishing company agreed to give it a second chance after the C.E.O.'s daughter loved the book. She had done this over a dozen times to get to that point.

Stephen King, a famous author, was so broke him and his wife worked multiple jobs and had to borrow clothes for their wedding. Also, they got rid of their phone because it was too expensive. King kept pursuing his craft writing and was continually getting rejected. He held up all of his rejection letters on his wall until the nail could no longer hold it. Then put up a stake (such a boss move). He finally sold his first short story for a mere $35, and after that, he wrote novels such as 'Carrie' and didn't receive much credit at first with only 13,000 copies being sold. However later on the rights bought out by a more prominent publishing company propelling King to eventually earning $200,000 for the same piece of writing.

Jim Carrey, famous actor/comedian, was struggling and living in a Volkswagen van outside a relative's lawn with his family and at age 15 began his career on stage but failed. He took this as a challenge though and committed so much that he quit school at 16 to pursue comedy full time. After that, would park in Mulholland Drive every night and visualize success and one day wrote himself a check for $10,000,000 for 'Acting Services Rendered' and dated it Thanksgiving 1995. Just before that very date, he got the job for the movie 'Dumb and Dumber' and hit that marker he wrote the check for.

Colonel Sanders, Founder of K.F.C., owned a gas station during the Great Depression but didn't have a restaurant. He would serve the diners around the area, later on, he perfected his recipe but lost his gas station. Was also only receiving at this point $105 every month from his pension and was stressed about the way life was going to go. He began sleeping in his car but was determined to franchise his chicken to a restaurant. He wanted a nickel for each piece of chicken sold. He was rejected more than 1,000 times before he finally met a partner.

Oprah Winfrey, legend, had to deal with such traumatic experiences from an early age. She has had to endure criticism and sexual abuse throughout her life and has even experienced some very extraneous burdens. Including her having a child at 14 and losing it two weeks later. She was repeatedly molested by her family and family friends, and through all of that hardship, she still managed to complete high school with honors and got a full academic scholarship to college where she began slowly but surely working her way up until she eventually created 'OWN,' her very own television network.

The reason those particular stories stood out to me

most is that they indeed paint a picture in your mind about perspective and the power of what we're actually able to do versus what we are currently doing. Most people get into such a state of comfortability that they are never even challenged to grow. Look at all of the above examples though and really just how much hardship they had to endure and how much adversity they needed to overcome that it almost didn't even seem as though they had a choice.

That's what makes them so iconic. These individuals were able to see the vision for themselves and pursue it beyond all odds. Why? Because even if they did fail, they knew that inside and deep down, if each of them had never made it, they would still be much happier going after it, then ever getting the reward right away. It sounds cheesy to say it is about the journey, but it truly is. Even if money is your objective in life, the mission is to accumulate wealth through the journey. Not just reach all of the money in the world at the start. You'll lose that money real quick. It all comes down to progression.

What ways are you propelling forward and not back? Up and not down. How are you growing each day to better yourself, the belief you have, and the willingness to pursue the dreams you've always imagined in your mind. This is the first step, so don't deter. You will not figure it out at the beginning, it will be confusing, but the key to consider is to stick with it. Just as all the others did in the examples above. Stick with it and don't give up because you will be rewarded. Just ensure that you continually grow correctly in the process because if you are not continually learning new things, you will be overworking on old ideas and an old baseline for reference. Be innovative with intensity, but patient for the benefit. Be modest but take what is yours and be aggressive but kind in the approach to your journey.

We are all a product of our thoughts, and a considerable portion of that is predicated upon what we intake from things such as the environment and the people we are around. If you're exposed to negative then you, in turn, will mirror that negative. Have you ever noticed that misery loves company? Or when someone was sad that their puppy died, you, in turn, felt sad as well. Even though you had no idea who that puppy was or that they also got a new puppy. Well mirrored neurons are to blame, but basically, we just love to mimic others. When they yawn we yawn etc. This is why you need to audit the things you watch, listen to, read, and interact with on a daily and at times second to the second basis. Making small adjustments will help with this because you may need to make drastic changes to see or feel results you want to experience but what I can tell you is this auditing will tremendously have an impact on the way you begin this process and start to become passionate about it.

The road trip is what you get excited about when you have a long way to go, and the same goes for your journey. Make it an exciting one with lots of twists and turns. The more experiences you have under your belt, the more you can teach others all that you have learned. It will never be all for nothing, and that is just another part of growing to keep yourself agile and ready to take on the world every day.

E (Q) Motions

In a Psychology Today article posted by Marilynn Wei M.D., J.D. On September 11, 2017, According to a study published in the Proceedings of National Academy of Sciences, they found there are 27 different categories of emotions:

1. Admiration
2. Adoration
3. Aesthetic Appreciation
4. Amusement
5. Calmness
6. Entrancement
7. Excitement
8. Interest
9. Joy
10. Romance
11. Triumph
12. Sexual Desire
13. Satisfaction
14. Empathy For Pain
15. Anxiety
16. Awe
17. Awkwardness
18. Boredom
19. Confusion
20. Craving
21. Disgust
22. Envy
23. Fear
24. Horror
25. Nostalgia

26. Sadness
27. Sympathy

Notice that positive emotions outweigh negative emotions by one or two. It means we need to take note that there will be just as many negative and uncomfortable aspects of life just as there are blessings and optimistic views about life. This is why you need to audit your language and intake more positivity than negativity. Once you expose yourself to these ideas, the easier it will become to pick uplifting words to retell yourself as opposed to negative words and thoughts that will only put you down. You've got to stand guard of the mind and be wary of the souls' harmful intake. In addition to this you can start to develop a growth mindset and what will happen is you'll begin to view all of those very negative emotions as challenges to overcome, and so you start embracing them, and instead of seeing them for what they are, you see them for what they can become. So you adjust your sail accordingly and try a different route. Not everything is going to play out the way you'd like but if you can become emotionally intelligent enough to know when to feel what and how not to feel but stay attached and it will provide for a very sturdy and permanent foundational setting for your new roots to begin to form.

Experiment:

The next time you get angry or upset that traffic is taking so long tell yourself exactly how you are feeling and why you are mad. Then say 'I respect the feelings of anger'

Breathe and respond accordingly;

- **Is there anything that can be done? Usually not.**
- **Can I control my reaction? Typically yes.**
- **Will it hinder my growth more to stay mad or let it go? Probably staying mad.**
- **Am I wasting time when I could be focusing harder on my dreams? Absolutely!**

According to a Forbes article published October 15, 2017, it states that thanks to a David Hawkins M.D., P.H.D., and his book Power vs. Force where it shows a person's log level, the measurable energy level in your magnetic field, increases with more positive emotions and literally died with negative. This means you are actually physically doing harm to your cells and destroying them with every bit of stress or anger, frustration, and sadness, just to name a few.

According to Travis Bradberry, Author of Emotional Intelligence 2.0, he states the only 36 percent of people can truly identify what they are feeling when they are feeling it. So that means the other 64 percent of people are merely having feelings and do not even know why or what those feelings are. Once you can identify what it is your feeling you can become entranced in that and begin to explore it. The more you can do that, the easier it becomes to control the reaction, and you can alter into logic and reason.

Being practical is a significant fundamental, so do not just assume since you control your emotions one minute now all of a sudden, you're a deemed Monk. This takes time and practice, and you may slip up every now and again. I certainly do. The goal is not to be so judgmental of yourself that you get intimidated because as far as what we just went over that would mean are killing more cells, no.

Instead, do the opposite and love yourself enough to accept that you are not perfect, but in acknowledging it, you become much closer to it.

It sounds crazy, I know, but you can trust me, the less you think about perfection as the key, the more perfect and effortless your life will become to you.

How I Do It

It took me quite a while to come into my own and figure out how to control my emotions. This is probably one of the hardest in my life that I've had to do, but here's what I do every single time I get a negative emotion or something that generally would sway me:

I identify what I'm feeling even if it's out loud. Acknowledgment means respect, and once I realized my emotions needed that they quickly turned into my friends and were willing to help me solve the problem as opposed to disagreeing all the time. You'll always hear that in relationships, the best and most effective tools are communication and compromise. So if you can do both with your emotions every time, even if they're positive, then you can form a great relationship with them and really get to know them.

Whenever I feel sad instead of getting even sadder about it, I explore deeper and try to figure out how we can go about this issue, much like a disagreement between a husband and wife. After I do this typically by the time I get back into the real world from my thoughts, the feelings have pretty much dissipated, and I can go about my day as usual. Being mindful of all of this can dramatically increase how you act and react to anything that goes on in the day.

Good or bad.

Emotions are a part of you and are comprised of a mix of different beliefs, perspectives, energies, environments, and elements all at play. Knowing this, people still use this as a form of decision making and react according to their state of emotion. Most people don't so much as think twice about which emotions are being felt. This is not to be confused with gut feelings, because those are based upon a different factor which is contingent upon being emotionally in tune. Anyone can say, "My gut tells me I should eat more ice cream." The fact of the matter, though is emotions will want to drive you, such as a child wanting to take the wheel. It just isn't smart.

Once you've created a solid foundation in which you can identify your feelings without giving them too much attention this will allow for the kind of detachment that won't hinder, but further, your understanding that some of them may have been programmed habitually due to circumstance or a traumatic event. Examples of this can be things like PTSD or addictions. Not having control over your emotions will allow for them to be the driving force behind your decisions and create habits in life you may have never intended on. The sooner you get more in touch with these emotions by acknowledging them and identifying why you feel specific ways, the sooner you will begin to free yourself of the undesired emotions slowly.

It has always astounded me how people could act so happy when they get what they want yet so stirred and so upset when things are going disastrous. It amazes me because of the lack of awareness in the current state. Some people naturally assume that because something is going right, it will continue that way.

Meanwhile, others in a downward spiral feel as though

climbing out is impossible, and so the search continues for answers as to why things are not aligned. The thing people fail to realize though is that nothing is permanent. Not our circumstance, and not even death as much as we like to believe. We disintegrate into the soil and/or are scoured among the wind into the air and are put back into the very existence in which we were created.

So what is it that is supposed to be done about not swaying too far to one side? Well, let's take a step back. Emotions are a part of you. So this means that the driving forces are a makeup of the things you're exposed to. The environment, the beliefs you have, and your formed perspectives on life. To achieve emotional stability, you should be able to acknowledge when you feel a particular emotion and identify why you are feeling the way that you are. Feelings must be respected enough to speak with them almost as a friend.

Have you ever noticed when you need help with a math problem you ask someone, and then sometimes as you explain how to do it out loud you figure out the correct answer? The same applies to emotion. Acknowledging the issue or problem can sometimes allow for clarification. The stronger and more stable your foundation of control, the easier all of it will come together in times of crisis. The problem is that only a few will actually apply this strategy. Practice makes perfect, but most will take it as words on a page and nothing more.

As Jericho is trying to make the last ten miles, he gets struck by everything all at once. He realizes that after this, he still has an entire 49 miles more to go. It is hard to hold onto the faith. Tired, extremely exhausted and weak, Jericho's spirit is now frail, and energy is low. Doubting himself far more than ever before. Who was he kidding? Why is he doing this? Was he trying to create this self-fulfilling prophecy? Now not only is he questioning his existence, but questions why he is even there. Should he turn back? The others didn't have it as rough as him growing up, so how would they know what he's going through. The conflict keeps growing, and he feels as though he's bashing his head against an imaginary wall. Above all, why was he talking to himself like this? The exhaustion and lack of water perhaps? Should he have just quit while he was ahead?

His truth began to fail him, all he is seeing now is the obstacle and not the beauty. What beauty has there indeed been when the amount of suffering becomes amplified so much more when it does happen? He is officially closed down at this point and is almost sure that he is going to stop after this part of it all. He cannot do another 57 miles, there's no way! At that moment, he stopped.

Something came over him during that very second. A flashback to the dream he had where he was suffering and fearful of death due to his broken spirit and lost faith. Just as he did when he was dreaming about the marathon, noticed a silhouette. Just as he began to shout, he saw that it was, in fact, somebody running up to him. He tried belting out, but nothing came out because his mouth was so dry. Instead, the man came up to him and said, "Oh boy, you're barely

alive out here!" He continued on, "Come on, man, you're seriously not that much further, let's go." Filled with more positive energy, he felt recharged a bit. Enough to take on the rest. During the last few miles, he had listened to the man reiterate all that he had been through before this race and how he has been able to do it every year for the last 9 years.

Jericho and his new mentor were able to finish the race and just in time for some food and some water with some incredible music and rest to follow. Upon going to sleep that night, Jericho truly pondered how everything played out. He reflected on the dream and how everything had all come together for him to create a breakthrough moment, such as that. Feeling strongly about that notion because Jericho had never believed in coincidences and always knew there was a grand design behind it all. He regained his level of empathy and began strengthening all of the bonds he had built so far. They reminded him to let go and enjoy all of the progress everyone has made. Tomorrow would be the last big haul before the final steps, and he was quite baffled at how much little there seemed to be left with all that he'd been able to achieve so far.

Part V: Purpose & Awareness

Stage Five: The Long March

This was it. This was the longest stretch yet. 49 miles as opposed to the others that were roughly 30. Jericho surviving through these circumstances was an understatement. He had just come through the hardest and roughest day yet. There were only two choices, stop now or press on. It got harder, but he got stronger, the land was tedious, but the night sky was exciting. He had lived through the 'try or die trying' mantra he had looped in his head. The highway to hell, and now this was going to be the roughest terrain. He was already broken and beaten down. He really debated on quitting due to the pain from the infections still plaguing both of his feet now. He was hurting, sore, exhausted, and dehydrated, to say the least.

One thing he had noticed though was, as he was looking for his mentor, everyone was talking with each other. Not moping in a corner by themselves.

Why was he so distraught? Well for one, he was isolated from everyone, damaging the ego into cowering instead of powering, and two, he had only actually gotten to know the mentor. He began to join in on some of the light witted banter going about the groups. He couldn't help but laugh at a few jokes from the other newbies and then was utterly in spirit during a veteran runner's last minute speech.

As he was listening, he took one final look around and was just basking in the glory of so much diversity all for one purpose. To help each other at this moment become believers. Believers in themselves, and believers in the fact that this is much bigger than a mere race. This is a symbol of how you combat daily life. Are you looking for instant gratification or a fulfilling journey that you can be proud to have had the privilege of taking? Jericho decided to choose the privilege option because regardless of how much agony he may have felt, he also felt honored throughout the entire experience. Yes, anger, doubt, fear, frustration, pain, but also honor. To carry out what he had set out to accomplish. Only now the real desire became to finish with more friendships built, more amazing views that will have been imprinted and the magical time travel that happens during the trek through some of the most ancient history and diverse terrain. Just as the group did, the entire marathon all had a different background and looked as though it came from different places. Just as the race is designed to create an inner

transformation, everyone that comes goes for the same purpose. Jericho has now been exposed to not only others, but experiences, and has cultivated a new level of empathy. The fact that each person had their own struggles, that meant the more they can all come together to allow belief. That is powerful. That's what got him through to this point. The power of the presence within his own self-belief. He is now all in and knowingly applying deep conscious awareness of gratitude for the journey, momentum from discipline, energy to keep moving, and the empathy to not only help others on the way but allow for help from others on the way to the finish line. He is aware that it is a group effort and the goal is to help everyone cross the finish line during this last 49-mile bout.

The Long March is a long March because most of it is desert plains with rough, challenging dunes entering into what is known as the moon valley. During this time it is absolutely all mental, Jericho feels the fear of everything he'd faced coming full blast but keeps powering through. He decided to bring in some of the positive trigger habits he was able to form before this second to the last stage. If he did not do this, it could very quickly become a vicious cycle of negativity bashing him in the head just as the heat was. Or weighing him down even more than his wrapped up shoes. This part was becoming insanely tricky but in the midst of it all still yet again were some incredible rock formations which allowed him to re-center. It's as though everything he has gone through so far; the water leak, the infection, the constant headaches of comparison and ego telling us not to carry out all the way to the finish, were all just roadmaps leading him to

the end. Only now he was able to do it while indeed gaining ultimate perspective resulting from his own curiosity. His willingness to ask the questions for himself, to himself. To achieve that more profound level of understanding within his own spirit to remain poised in this final match with fear itself. It has all been leading up to this moment, and all he has to do is keep putting one foot in front of the other.

23 hours went by, and at the last checkpoint before the final footsteps, he ran in and received instant hugs and high fives. It felt nice to get that level of acknowledgment for only finishing that part. Later that night, everyone all gathered around a fire, telling jokes and stories. Reflecting upon all of the new discoveries people found within themselves. It was at that moment, Jericho knew and felt full for the first time in his life, like he was in the right place at the right time. Fully embracing who he is and knowing that this moment is as it is supposed to be.

Awareness for Ourselves

"What works for me doesn't necessarily work for you."
- Gary Vaynerchuck.

Our mind is one of the most incredible pieces of human intelligence. It controls everything from your senses to how we think and perceive things to being able to execute the desired task. However, it is most often not used correctly or ever a sought over desire. Money usually is. If you were to ask people if they would instead take a smarter brain or more money, the majority would probably go for the money. Failing to realize that with a more improved brain, the notion of money is substantially not as appealing knowing you'd have all the potential in the world to make a buck. The idea that mind over money is composed of investing in your own self and growth.

If you were to start building a house before a foundation is set, well then there is no house for long. Same goes with us as human beings. We cannot expect to soar without first creating a base. A rocket cannot take off without being attached to a sturdy base to hold it.

Now that the idea behind mind over money's opening your own mind to visions and dreams. Don't feel as though you are limited, just feel, and list all of the things you'd like to become or do. Without the need for money. Money is a tool, a real piece of paper utilized as an exchange of something of equal value. So the idea that money is what you need makes no sense because the amount of money you spend is in exact proportion with where you are in life. So the more money you want to spend the less time you'll have to spend it and vice versa. Money can either be a negative influence or positive affluence in which you use it to excel further into your future and your vision.

Majority of the time, however, money is detrimental because it is sought for the wrong reasons, or the ones that obtain it are not ready. The ones that have built empires such as Jeff Bezos, Gary Vaynerchuk, Tony Robbins, and Jay Shetty are the ones that utilize the money for positive. They all realized early on that it isn't about the money, but rather what the money can do that intrigued them.

They had their self-awareness and passion early on and just knew how to make marginal adjustments to their plan to adapt to the realization that money was the tool, not the reward.

If money is your reward, it's like saying you can survive on drugs. The supply will be endless, and there will be no end, but with fragile self-discipline, what is that doing to your health? If you are ungrateful for the five dollars in your pocket right now, you definitely won't be grateful hundreds, thousands, or even millions.

Negatives are like weeds, if you don't do the maintenance in the yard, they will form quickly and obnoxiously. We need to take responsibility and be humble at the fact that it is us that needs to clean these weeds and nobody else can. Bringing this sense of ownership will spark a new sense of pride in that newfound responsibility. No matter what gets poured onto us, whether it be hardship, loss, or failure, we need to think of ourselves as seeds getting dirt and soil poured onto us. Then with adequate nourishment, which is your acceptance, we intake all of the bad that reigns upon us, and we begin to grow like a seed from the ground. Seeds start off in the dirt and become beautiful flowers, plants, and trees. The same could be said for us as human beings. So take the negatives with a winning attitude because this can make or break your confidence, and confidence is always the key.

This is extremely important in execution and belief. If you cannot set up goals for yourself and actually reach them, things will probably seem hopeless. This is the case for most people. They set a goal, cannot achieve it, and do not attempt again. The key is to fail often because that is the road to success. The more we fail, the more naturally we learn from mistakes. Evolving and learning each step of the way. It isn't enough in the year 2019 to simply work hard. It's much more complicated than that. It is about the idea of working hard and smart in harmony. It is this combination that will provide for a middle ground sense of being and can open your eyes to new possibilities and opportunities.

If you are just not reaching your goals then reevaluate, don't just give up. Make marginal adjustments to either your routines or the goal itself and begin to start pinpointing the places in which you are lacking and either hire someone or find someone to do certain things to free up your time to get it done. Or just take it down a notch and build momentum to push past all of the disbelief and roadblocks along the way.

The only way you can see the actual transformation is if you go with the current and do not fight it. If you can learn to adapt and adjust, then you will get to where you want to be much quicker. Persistence is how water can go around things and not through them. Do you have any idea how much effort it takes to stop water completely? Try maybe five years and $49 million. That's how much it effort it took to build and put up the Hoover Dam. So unless you have five years to waste and are a billionaire, I do not think you should try to fight to stop the currents in your life when you could save the time and effort for you to build wealth and create more abundance from traveling through to your destination as opposed to walking.

You may only get halfway there due to dehydration and malnutrition. At least with water, you have the momentum in your favor. So ride the seas and learn the shifts. It will all be worth it in the end.

Patience

Patience is critical in drawing this out long term and making it practical. You first need to become very self-aware and isolate what you're good at. Typically your passion coincides with this because whatever you feel passionate about is what you tend to work harder and longer on. So the work doesn't feel like work. Whenever you were a child, I'm sure you were told to dream, right? Reach for the stars, and as we get older, the mindset tends to shift. It goes from being a growth mindset to being a fixed mindset.

As we get older, we are told to get a practical job and to go to school and go into debt and work until you retire and pay the debt off and then live happily ever after when this couldn't be further from the truth. What those very people won't tell you is that they've already stopped dreaming and that conforming is what you should do because they did it. These are also the same people strolling through Facebook or Instagram all day comparing their lives with others. It is toxic. Remove yourself from that and do not be scared to live for your dream.

The reason patience matters is because when you're not where you want to be three years from now, you are okay that you still have more work to do. When you are not where you want to be ten years from now, you've already given up three times over and regret even more now because you didn't stay patient and poised in your pursuits.

Remain actively patient. Not just sitting around saying if you have hope, you'll be okay. It doesn't work that way. Life doesn't seem to work in the ways we think. So if you're a kid to 18, don't worry about what you want to do with your life. Just keep experimenting and find out what you really love to do. When you're 19 to 21, you start to form what you love and realize you actually do have a practical approach to acknowledging it. Then from 22 to the unforeseen future, you work for whatever it is you decided on with complete aggression. It doesn't happen overnight. There is no such thing as overnight celebrities. It takes real famous people you know roughly 10 years to make it. Some a little less but all of them had to out tremendous amounts of work in. Work that neither of us would be willing to do.

Another difference between the truly fulfilled and successful people in life is that they to the extra mile every time. There isn't a moment they feel they should slack or not carry their best selves forward each day. It will take time, and you will get impatient, but this is when you need to stick with it and feel within yourself that beyond this is what you desire. Do not fold under the influence of laziness and indulgence. Instead, savor the abundance and sacrifice present to make it that much sweeter.

Do not be mistaken though you need to work at hyper speed for this process to work. You need to figure out what the ten-year plan is and work vigilantly and tirelessly on that goal. Make every decision quickly and don't waste time trying to figure out every little detail of every little thing. It's okay to be meticulous but not to the point where you're more focused on scheduling than actual effort and merit you are putting into the intended target.

The more you do not do now, the more you will have to regret in the future. That much is obvious, but there is no way around the actual work. Patience plays a significant role because you need to be able to instill it for the practical side of what you're wanting to do. It allows you not to rush what you're doing but create value in what you're wanting to do. So that way it's coming from a genuine, authentic place and people aren't just seeing someone trying to take more of their time. Time is the most valuable asset in life, so don't waste others. It can be challenging to be patient, but do it. Practice daily. Nothing worth it is easy and nothing easy is worth it. Both life and the universe have a tendency to reward the tenacious doers for their substantial merit.

The sooner we can realize that the mind is what acts as the decision maker over all that we do the better view we have of the importance of taking care of it properly. Right now I bet you feel as though as soon as you put this book down, you will go back to whatever habits it is you were doing in the first place. If you think that way then, of course, you will. That's the beauty and the curse or what you are reading. It becomes a working habit that you need to exercise daily, but once you do, your entire focus will shift with it from unproductive things to productive things. So many people feel as though they are busy but get nothing done. Sure you just cleaned the whole house but at what cost of your time? Did you set yourself beforehand for after the cleanup? What is the plan for the rest of the week? Most people don't have the next few hours planned, let alone ten years. It's essential to prepare for what you can. Preparation allows for practicality to flourish because trial and error is hand in hand and synonymous with failure to plan correctly. It is a baseline for which you can reference as you see fit to identify the mistakes made or the inaction taken.

How to Change Habits

What habits do you have? Perhaps it's too much ice cream or television. Maybe too much eating and not enough exercise. Smoking and drinking? Or drugs. Regardless of what it is. There are a few things we can use as a reference tool belt to help counteract the ineffective habits and replace them with productive, healthy habits. First off the thing to do is identify why. Why are you doing this, and what drives your habits? Is it avoidance of something? Is it because you feel you don't deserve greatness in your life? Is it just too hard to get out of bed every morning, so you need to drink that bottle to make life tolerable? Or maybe you're absolutely at peace, but you get these terrible moments of loneliness and depression.

Identify what it is that is making you feel this way. The sooner and more honest you can be with yourself, the more this will help.

Next, after you've identified it, you cope with it. What steered you down this path? Forgive that event or forgive yourself for just making bad decisions. It's EXTREMELY VITAL to forgive yourself because you need to realize we are not perfect no matter how hard we try. Neither are others. We seem to have it in our heads that perfection is something attainable, so we use influence as a reference, and when we cannot live up to that expectation no matter how unrealistic, we get down on ourselves and feel we are not worth it so why try.

Once you've pinpointed why then we can move onto triggers. What are triggers allowing this to continue? Is it stress, sadness, nobody to talk to? Whatever it is identify it much like the why factor. Then once you've done that learn where the environments are in which you are exposed to this most. Is it around friends? Work? Family? If it is one of these, you need to do your best in reducing or eliminating the time taken out for these. It goes back to auditing, people and the environment play a huge role in our energy levels. Are the places or people you are associating yourself with draining energy or feeding it? I don't mean completely disconnect with everyone around you but more of a harmonious detachment. More so detaching the associating tendencies and leaving the emotional responses at the door.

So the best way to do this would be in the following example;

You have a coworker that gossips on and on at the local bar you two go to after work, you begin drinking more frequently and realize it's getting worse, so you want to stop. How do you stop when your friend has no issues but still wants to continue to do that because it's their form of stress release and is not an unhealthy excess? The best way to go about this would be to talk and say you are going to cut back so and you are going to start hitting the gym after work. Perhaps you can go for drinks afterward. Typically the friend will not want to wait; however, you still take the friends feelings into account. If they do decide always to want to go for drinks after the gym then simply call and say you are exhausted. Most of the time it isn't the bond nor any friendship at stake here but merely another way to go about a situation to set yourself up for success and allow others to see what you're capable of. You can always disconnect entirely and let them know you are done and to not bother you regarding drinks or those types of things but just because some argues with why you're doing it doesn't mean they are not your "true" friend. It just means they don't necessarily have time to understand all that you have learned.

There are many options to go about this, and if the habits are becoming extremely destructive then absolutely cut off the relationship entirely. Most often than not though it is merely something as little as watching too much TV though or being on the phone in the wrong ways too much. If there is someone that develops an addiction or you feel you are developing one do not hesitate to seek professional help because those are what can physically cause the brain not to see any issues with what you are doing. Some may be chemical imbalances so just be sure you can control over your mind to reiterate the earlier part of this chapter. It isn't about money, or all of the fancy cars are clothes. Is your head right, healthy, and ready? Those are the fundamental questions you need to ask yourself when attempting fulfillment in life.

Progress Is Process

"If you can take care of today, ten years from now will take care of itself." - Tom Bilyeu

So much like what was just covered above. The idea that the process produces results, or what I call progression, is what has always astounded me. To obtain a good result, you must first get progress. The same goes for the opposite, to have a negative effect, you must contain regression. Remember, life is cunning, but that is part of what makes it so beautiful. In essence, if you are going throughout the day and doing more regressive than progressive well, then it can be easier to identify specific issues. So if for example, you are wanting to become a CEO of a company one day, then all of your decisions throughout the day need to be a proactive reflection of that. You cannot want to be a CEO and not do more than you did the day before. It just is not even theoretically possible. The less you do each day, the less you become. Much like the less you eat of your daily nutritional value intake, you begin to lose weight. Remember, growth weighs more than mistakes. Your muscle weighs more than your fat. Think of fat as mistakes. You learn from your fat and burn it, creating micro tears to produce more muscle tissue. Do this for your growth in life as well.

If you are doing your best every single day for the next five to ten years, where will you be? What could you become? The possibilities are literally endless, and people feel as though there is no place for them in this world. So many have gone on thinking the earth is this scary and dark place full of negativity. Well, it is, but what it can be if you allow it is abundant, beautiful, glorious, illuminated, and positive. The outlook ultimately depends on your inner state. Referring back to harmonious detachment, think about the balance between the good and the evil. There is no one over the other because the power of contrast allows us the grace of being able to be thankful and grateful for both states of mind. It is in recognition of this that we can truly begin to be at peace within ourselves and propel the momentum further.

The first step to beginning your own journey of progression is by starting. By doing, and by taking massive action and not giving a crap about what anyone else thinks or what anyone else wants or what you are doubting. It's about beginning your journey or newfound purpose and creating a meaningful and fulfilling life you can look back and say, "I'm not rich, but I have a rich life." I want that for you, and I want you to want that for you also.

Conversation over Signature

Remember it's about the conversations. It's about the substance. I've always been the type that feels as though the content is what allows for consistency. When things contain something you absolutely have a passion for then, it is much easier to stick with it and continue to keep it fresh and creative. All of the people you follow that talk about self-development and going on the journey make their content have substance, and this is what is intriguing to us about them. It is because they can take the material to a different level in this conversation.

Most people view the signature as a stamp. Their approval branded in and now they just need to sign here, sign there. Absolutely not. Think about life as a meeting, but at the end of this meeting is our eternal resting place. Are you going to want to skip to the end of that meeting, sign your life away and simply die? No! You're going to want to stick around and listen to the entire conversation to prolong the eventual fate which is you signing away your life.

Don't get mistaken by the money or the fancy things. The money is a byproduct. We get too caught up in the signature that we forget what it took to achieve these things. Life is about the small moments that you create within that meeting. The funny jokes you make, the productivity of it as a whole. It all comes down to what you decide to talk about, substance.

Do your best every day, and the entirety of life will consist of amazing, fulfilling moments. You ever notice how your favorite singers' album has so many beautiful songs it's hard to pick one? Make different parts of your experiences themed and capture a collage of treasured scenes from your life in a compilation of moments.

It is never too late or too early to start or end something. Either we try to give ourselves this excuse that if we would have only started sooner than we would have more time. Well, you're not wrong, but the fact of the matter is nobody has more time. We all have a set amount of time but don't focus on the regret focus too much instead on the now. What you can do now will trump anything you've done in the past, whether good or bad, and it only becomes multiplied in the future. All you've got to do is start to isolate which parts you are feeling in life and be honest with yourself.

This is where people have such a hard time. They are not honest with themselves. Most people don't tell themselves the hard truths and really ask conscious questions about their existence. Time is our asset, and we need to leverage it accordingly. We all only have 24 hours the difference between you and the person you are admiring or trying to emulate is what they choose to do within those allotted hours.

Have you ever stopped to see what a typical day is for the life of your favorite person? Look at their daily routine, and I guarantee you could not follow it. Why? Because the process is what matters. The most successful people in the world love the substance, the in-between and unsure, the parts of life in which they weren't sure where the meal was coming from. They loved every part of the journey, including the worst parts. It's because they had a belief that they held true within their hearts and decided it was loved so much they'd rather be homeless trying to reach it rather than regret not attempting it at all.

When you get that desire for something, do not steer away because someone tells you it isn't realistic. What's not realistic is you being friends with them after a comment such as that. What I mean though is who cares as long as it's practical to you because you've studied the day in and day outs of those things whatever it is, and you felt challenged and not intimidated. You didn't feel overwhelmed; you felt encouraged. That's what you need to realize and think to start to really move and keep the pace up.

Overnight success is an illusion. Fear is an illusion. Nobody ever got to where they are by giving in to the fear and letting the emotion tell them to stop. Danger and fear are different, and most people experience fear. This is why you need to realize that human potential is limitless. We can do things we never thought were possible, but we've lost such connection with our mind and body that we are unable to envision what we are truly capable of.

So many people believe that they will never get the thing they desire because they will fall short. Well, one of my favorite sayings is the one with the child falling continuously to learn how to walk, and it's a perfect example because you don't tell that child to stop trying to walk right? You encourage them to keep going and keep working at it. The same goes for us in these scenarios.

We need to do a better job of encouraging ourselves to keep going even if one thing didn't work out. Do not be afraid of being shy. Be the first one to go if somebody asks for volunteers. I always did these things so that I could be an example and plus if you go first you automatically have more experience than the others. It's all about how you view it. So realize your potential by knowing you can do great things as long as you have a great mindset. When you realize this, it's easier to visualize how far your reach can go. You figure out how much you're willing to sacrifice to fulfill this untapped potential and when that happens is when you get fired up and passionate about becoming better each and every morning you wake up. Once the reach happens and you begin to want to move, you utilize complete and total aggression and persistence in getting there.

It all encompasses the theme of a fulfilled life, which is progression. Progression has always been a critical component of my life. The one constant I could measure with and love every process with. It gave me the ability to break things down in a way enough to organize and write this book. These were all things I learned on my own and then had further strengthened and contextualized by other admirable people such as Tony Robbins, Jay Shetty,

Aubrey Marcus, Gary Vaynerchuck, Tom Bilyeu, Jim Kwik, Grant Cardone, Dean Graziosi, Ed Mylett, Jim Rohn, Will Smith, just to name a few!

Every single one of these people will also tell you it's about the conversation. Another way to view this would be to take the entirety of your life. Everyone wants to skip to the end where they have all of the money, the cars, and the clothes but at what point will you begin to value now?

Value today and the breaths coming in and out of your lungs as you read this book. The conversation also allows for opportunities in meeting new people or finding something out or maybe being there at the exact right moment. Whatever it is though you need to be present, and everyone is different in the ways that they view this. For me, however, this was the thing I still need to work on. It is a challenge to remain patient, but the actively patient ones always win. Active patience means playing the long game strategically. Once you realize this, everything comes together because you know that you have all of your control today and have the power to dictate your tomorrow.

Patience Is Passion

"There is no greatness without a passion for being great, whether it's the aspiration of an athlete or an artist, a scientist, a parent, or a businessperson." - *Tony Robbins*

Lastly, Passion, my favorite. This is the one that people tend to overthink, but for me, there has always been nothing to think about. What do you love? Whatever it is we have the luxury of living in a life now where anything can become a career or enjoyed hobby loved by thousands if not millions. This was not always the case, but if you love your kids share your life on platforms such as YouTube, Instagram, or Snapchat. Start a dog walking business via Facebook and see where that goes and perhaps start a podcast talking about sports. Maybe just a simple blog about any of these subjects you know to get things out can change the way you think about what it is to have passion for something.

If you have yet to find a passion and or purpose do not stress. It is not hard to find, nor is it far away. Actually quite the opposite, it is nearby. Mostly in everything we do or are exposed to. Exposure in itself can be everything. You often hear celebrities talk about how they watched someone they admired on television or that they used to watch Michael Jordan and want to play like him. This could also be in a negative way, such as all you are exposed to is drugs, and therefore, you abuse them. Or maybe something even smaller such as your parents always speeding and you never seeing anyone go the speed limit, still five over typically, so you do the same. Another example could be growing up not so financially stable. You may have never had any idea of how to save let alone invest your money, time, and energy.

Much like having a fixed mindset, which we will go over along with the growth mindset in chapter three. The sooner you can pinpoint what it is that you love and be very specific, the sooner you can begin to revolve your life around a given purpose, and this propels growth and progression the most. This gives you the advantage over others because you don't mind putting in the relentless hours and discipline it takes to put your life into that next level, so to speak.

There are, however, other parts to it the shortcomings of the success. If you're very passionate but lack strengthened relationships, you will feel lonely. Your health will decline regardless, and we all experience the same fate, so it is imperative to take care of yourself. Exposure to certain parts of life, such as drugs, among other types of addictive behaviors can alter your perceptions, especially if you are still in the beginning stages of figuring out who you are.

To help with this, begin to notice the people that you look up to and see which ones are more fulfilled rather than not so much, and figure out which aspect is lacking. For most hip-hop artists, they have great relationships and passion, but they fall into the abyss of narcotics and some overdose or get into legal trouble because of their neglect towards health mentally and physically. The most successful hip hop artists have always used music as the passion and purpose, the ones you never hear anymore are the ones that used money as the passion or purpose. It becomes toxic. Observing the differences between someone working and having all of the cash versus someone internally fulfilled without any money at all is quite impressive. The thing people misconstrue is their concept of what success is. People have such a hard time imagining themselves in the future because they can barely get through the present. The future becomes an opaque blur, much like space did long ago.

It isn't enough to just say all you need is a passion, what this takes are trial and error. What you're passionate may not always be what you're good at so you may need to practice and get good at the thing you love, but if you genuinely love it, you will stick it out and push through. That's the beauty about revolving your life around your passion, it will, in turn, become your purpose. That notion alone brings satisfaction to our inner self. Knowing that we are giving back, doing something we love is the most fulfilling thing you can do.

There's no price for helping people become better and doing good for others for no reason. Everybody wants to take, take, take but the more you receive from others, the more you'll have to give in order to get it. You need to establish a relationship first with people and help them to build it before you can ask for things. I never ask for most anything unless it's a must. Like when my family and I were getting evicted because we couldn't afford rent, obviously you need to find a place to stay so you ask. There is a power to the asking, but there is no power in taking handouts. Nor is there any pride in it. There is also a considerable difference between pity and help but do not get mistaken by ego and think logically in these situations. If it compromises anything about you, do not take it, but if it makes sense and you can leverage that then, by all means, go for it.

Leverage is a power in itself that we will go over but mostly what is essential here is that you identify with who you are at the core, and never be ashamed of who you are. You can be anything you want, so explore and find what it is that sparks your soul the way that you need to get going and begin getting excited about life's possibilities!

The goal of this book is to open that spectrum. Do not worry if you haven't found what you love yet. The keyword is "yet." When you can find a purpose, this is what gives your life meaning. This is what allows you to wake up and know you have a place in this world because the truth and the fact of the matter is, you do have something to contribute. The goal of this last section is not to have you figure out precisely what it is that you are going to do, but rather enhance your awareness that in the end, this is the last pillar to complete the cycle of fulfillment. So now to further your understanding of this concept of finding your purpose, let's move on to the process.

Harmonious Rhythm

"Happiness is not a matter of intensity but of balance, order, rhythm, and harmony." -Thomas Merton

Harmonious rhythm is when everything is working together cohesively and can perform at a consistent, optimum level. It is harmony within the realm of happy and sad. Good and evil, if you will. Those moments in life when you can feel the happiness within you radiate outward and you notice time begins to slow almost as if a Hallmark movie is playing in the background. Those moments when you realize that you are enjoying every second of it and trying to back in it for as long as you can. So what is it that is causing distress in your life? Could it be bills, a spouse, a career, or emotions in general? What about loss or maybe somebody hammering down at you to figure out what you're doing with your life? Or perhaps you just have no guidance whatsoever but have all of these thoughts and ideas rushing through your head and cannot even attempt at trying to tame them. However, the key is not to control them. Whatever it may be, I can tell you that I've been there, and I've felt the anger and frustration mixed with sadness and loneliness, while maintaining happiness but almost at in a false way.

Feelings are feelings, and as discussed in the chapter with emotions, all we can do is acknowledge and respect them, which will, in turn, control them instead of the other way around. Now, with that being said, when you reflect on the belief chapter as well, it will be found that the environment and people can influence what doubt is portrayed on you. This is where typically some people can fall into a trap.

Let's say you do the exercises with emotion and belief, and you're feeling good. Then, all of a sudden to do so you cut off the toxic people in your life. You finally come to a realization that there's nobody around you. This is not always the case. See, as in the empathy part, you need healthy relationships with the people that care about you and that build you up to carry out any sort of fulfillment. Many people, including celebrities can feel depressed and alone due to these same combinations of factors of not just relationships, but any of the baselines gone over in this book. It is not that you need to just completely cut out the people you love, go all in on some crazy diet, or pretend like everything's okay when it isn't.

Sometimes it may not be their fault because of what their beliefs are limited to, that diet isn't cohesive to what you want, or that you just felt putting on that front was the right thing to do.

Regardless of any of these, you cannot isolate yourself to loneliness and expect to have or develop excellent personal and social skills. Which are vital to both communication and networking, especially in the year 2019. What you've got to learn instead is my own personal technique in dealing with this issue.

I needed help dealing with associated emotional stability and intelligence. I basically did not know how to go about feeling what I was feeling, and it was causing too much disharmony in my life. I would be overly stressed and constantly worried. Anxiety would find me all of the time, and I wouldn't deal with it but instead act as though I had it all figured out. See when we do this it is out of our desire to have the answers and not find the answers. If we haven't looked into the depths of who we are, then we haven't yet figured out why we're feeling the way we're feeling.

Once you target specific emotions, you can identify the triggers. If I am feeling mad all of the time and I can analyze the anger over engaging with it, then that is half the battle. From there, you can detach and begin to take these personalized connotations for every event that takes place in your life. Let's discuss more specifically detachment and isolation.

According to a study done by Chapman University back in 2017, of the top fears of Americans, the first five included government pollution, American healthcare, of oceans, pollution of drinking water or not having enough money for the future. The idea that the anxiety of society is so predicated on external things leaves anyone vulnerable to that same level of thinking. Remember not to fear but embrace and take head on everything you ever thought impossible. Regardless of what you may believe we are, in fact, in a different generation where we are no longer helpless to the nine to five but can make other ways of income.

Rewards with Carelessness

When you receive rewards for merit, the ego is awarded as well. This can either have a detrimental effect or a very humbling effect on life. One can earn money and begin to forget why he or she started. Looking at it from an outside perspective, it seems obvious, however being on the inside of it, you cannot always tell the difference. When you are humbled in your learnings and wise in your teachings, you listen more than talk.

Most people are quick to jump the gun about when to speak. Be silent unless spoken to. Or unless the knowledge is giving someone direct value. While not caring what others think is the objective still at least be empathetic to the people less fortunate than you. Do not compete with anyone but yourself and do not compare yourself to others. Don't lose footing at the cost of a dollar. The value of a dollar goes down every day, but the things you learn and the self-improvement taught to yourself will never lose value unless you don't apply them.

Action and speaking are two totally different things. Once you can identify and begin to work more than you speak and listen to talk when necessary than you've become very humble. It's when the voice of the ego wants recognition that the carelessness begins to draw out, but when you can silence the Id, the ego will quiet, and you can focus on getting back to what the ultimate goal is. Being careless will get you to a place you don't want to be exceptionally quick, but you wouldn't notice until it is too late, so begin to identify if you are seeking the reward of achievement and progression or just use that to 'make it rain' in the club every night.

Harmonious Stability

The key is creating harmony within yourself. So it may not be in the order of this book, but there are few critical traits in which I'm sure you identify with most. Take the ones that you know you need help with and learn how to apply them to the already existing. Just because it isn't broken doesn't mean it cannot be improved. If you're not continually finding ways to grow and become better much like a business someone else will, and they will surpass you. Someone always has it worse, and someone is still working harder, that's just the reality.

People think they are entitled to admiration and status without putting in any of the work and creating an account and calling themselves a guru all of a sudden puts ten plus years under their belt. The world does not owe you anything, and the majority of it will not push you or even seem as though they care about the minute details of your life. This is why you've got to have this foundation set and have harmony in place. Nothing can throw you off your game, and if it does well, then you've got the tools necessary to compete and fight back being harmoniously humble.

People are not realistic. They go from having nothing and being broke, to wanting to do absolutely no work and receive passive income while sitting on a beach in Mexico. This depiction is the furthest thing from accurate because there is no dream to sell. The beauty is the presence within the journey. The selling is the day in and day outs. Life is truly an investment of time, energy, and dedication to receive all of the benefits within yourself.

Did you ever notice how wealthy people seem just to throw money around and still seem to have more? It's because they work more than they spend. You just only see the spending. Even working 23 and a half hours a day means you'd only have to make a ten-minute clip minimum about how you blew money at a bar. Yet people attribute that this ten minute glorified new story is the way their lives are 24/7. I can tell you for sure it isn't. Work more than you play, and the money problems seem to fade away. Get lost in your passion; that's why the last part of this cycle is so important. Without desire and purpose, we are a driven species without a destination, and that leads to so many wrong roads taken.

False Reality

From birth, we have painted this picture from everyone of how the world is supposed to be. So right from the get-go, we have been programmed to be the person that your mother or father wanted. It isn't because they wanted the worst for you. It's because they wanted the best for you. Then as you got older, you were able to take those truths they gave you along with societal facts your friends had and were able to form the reality we see here today.

This truth could be formed on the unstable ground though, and if you feel as though your world is crashing down upon you well, then it doesn't mean there's anything wrong with you. It just means there's something that wasn't placed right during the construction, so the foundation was cracked. That led to other problems becoming more significant and eventually resulting in the house being demolished, but that's okay! Why? Well, because the new foundation is being set and now there will be no cracks. If there are any issues, it will be easy to pinpoint the fix.

Now the reason the foundation cracks is because we are all sold this idea that the meaning of life is to go to school, get a job, work hard, get married, have a family and then retire. This can paint for a very unrealistic picture and is not a practical outlook, but it seems genuine. However, this is not the case.

Consider the economic crash in 2008. Everyone lost jobs, 401k accounts, and everything in between. You cannot rely on the banks, and you cannot rely on a fabricated, false picture of reality. On the flip side to that, we are in a digital age that is only expanding in which people are still being sold contrasted levels of extreme. Becoming exposed to YouTube and Instagram influencers, making actual money, people are taught to believe that they put up one video and or post, and all of a sudden, it's going to happen overnight. Or that simply the material things are what it's about.

It isn't about making millions and getting the attention of everyone in the world, and it isn't about settling and scrounging your whole entire life, it is about finding balance and harmony in what you see as the perfect reality for yourself. This is an age where we can indeed be who we want to be and can let the market decide what they think of it. This is where it can get tricky, instead of pretending you have this extravagant lifestyle, sit down, and just imagine what you are doing in the future. Can you picture it vividly? Most people cannot because they haven't taken the time to even correctly form the idea of what their ultimate reality should look like. They are so caught up in the lifestyle they don't see the merit behind the work, and are not fluent in the language of struggle so fail to notice or pay attention to the progression of how they've grown. Instead, they look at the finished product and think, 'oh I want to be that,' not knowing it may have too anywhere from 5 to ten years to build. Don't give in to a false sense of reality this is why lifelong learning is a must because the more you learn, the more you're able to form a true self-reality in which you're the creator and can dictate almost as if it were a lucid dream.

It looks as though the foundation is being set, and once that is in place, the building process begins. The idea behind all of the small ideas and strengthen belief along with emotions and even the Pillars themselves is to start becoming emotionally intelligent to some degree and allowing you to identify which parts of yourself are holding you back. The world isn't going to feel sorry for you, and nobody is going to feel sorry for your problems because everybody has them. The sooner you can take accountability instead of blaming people, or other factors learn to take ownership of the things that happen in your life, and I can promise the amount of growth you will see in yourself will triple. Learn to be grateful, someone will always have it worse than you! Once you get this new perspective, it's much easier to begin to visualize yourself in the future and start to cultivate that belief within you if you haven't yet.

"Fast-forward where you are. Look at yourself in 10, 15, 20 years' time and ask yourself the question: Is that where I want to be? If you're in a company, look at that person who's 20 years ahead of you and ask yourself: Is that where I want to be? If you're in a start-up, look at where other startups have got to in similar roles and go: Is that where I want to be? And if the answer's NO, then you need to find a new path." - Jay Shetty

Humility Hero

"Humility is not thinking less of yourself, it's thinking of yourself less." -C. S. Lewis

Being a humility hero is being able to become familiar with the love of process. It is required to continue, I'm afraid. It always struck me how ordinary people felt the need to be extraordinary. What possessed them to commit such selfless acts for the good of others with no sort of compensation or validation? If you consider superheroes, they never knew where the situations or circumstances would take them, but what they always had faith in was that they were doing good for humanity or, the bigger picture.

When growing up, people would always know that I was a generous and an understanding person, so at times, some would take advantage of it, or at least that was what I was convinced. What I never understood was how other people could see that as a third party, though? Why did I not feel as though the people were taking advantage? That is when I realized I wanted to give much like the superheroes I grew up admiring.

My definition of taking advantage was different than others. The conditioned mind is a mighty discipline. We all have something to give to this world. For some it's art or creation, for others it's merely giving back. You may even be good at your job or at being a parent. If so notice these things. These are your superpower. Once you can identify your origin story and follow that with a point of realization, then all you need to do is have your plan of attack and proceed to execute.

For peter parker, it was the spider bite, For Dr. Strange, it was losing his talent as a surgeon. For The Incredible Hulk, it was the gamma radiation. For Captain America, it was the chamber that turned him into a super soldier. So this means once you open yourself up to, and engage in the practice of the ideas in this book, then you will begin to have that moment of clarity in which you can isolate what you're talents are to contribute to the betterment of society.

Once you can solve more problems in the areas of your field, you can begin to create value for yourself, and people become more open to you being the go-to person for whatever the need is in that category. It is crucial to think about and be self-aware in knowing who you are and what you are trying to do to help people. It isn't enough to simply use your powers for your own selfish gains. As Peter Parker's Uncle said,

"With great power comes great responsibility". - Stan Lee

As a new found hero, what is your first act of selflessness going to be? It is in these decisions where you either become a hero or a villain, using your powers for good or evil. This is when you can start to become the change. If you're a writer change the world through words if you're a singer change the world through song if you're a teacher change the world through guidance. If you're a good parent, change the world by shaping your children, and if you're a decent person, change the world by being a catalyst and an advocate for change. Just isolate your powers and focus on them until they are mastered but share the growth with people, and you can meet other heroes such as yourself and build your own Avengers team.

So here's where the theory gets exciting and has been tested and proven. Think of your favorite music artists. Each one has a unique style, flow, and swagger about them that makes them who they are. Same goes for any sport or any celebrity in the world. However, the same thing does apply to you because it applies to everyone. See much like in the comics everyone has the capabilities and the capacity for all of this. It's the few that actually do something about it that becomes something from it. There's a reason they wanted the superheroes to have unique but some very ordinary bio stories. There have even been real-life attempts at this done in movies such as "Kick-Ass" because it is widely known that humans have potential, but is untapped potential. Only through experience and application can if all unfold. This is truly important to know.

Experience comes from your everyday battles and learning every minute of those days. Apply more knowledge to combat every form of villain you have inside. That is the ultimate goal. Not peace. One thing is for, you've already been bitten! You've already got the untapped potential now all you have to do is become self-aware and know what your strengths and weaknesses are.

Once you've determined that, have a mission in place and set a purpose through the exploration of passion. Things will seem hard and grueling, but the sooner you can do this, the more you can face the more robust parts of life with a sense of urgency and not avoidance. We know what avoidance does, and we need to become courageous and step forward, much as Thor did with the hulk in the fantastic movie "Thor: Ragnarok."

You have to step up and take the throne. Only when you're ready will it be prepared for you. So face your fears and face the villains of your world and just know nobody is better than you and you are not better than anyone else. Everyone is equal, some have only tapped the potential sooner than others. You will experience what is called a paradigm shift. This is when you realize that your struggle is hard, grueling even. You want to relax, but your idea of relaxing is sitting on a couch not contributing in the slightest bit to society Pondering as to why you have no riches quite yet? Whatever your design is of relaxing, just know that applied to everyone is the idea that if we do not grow, we shrink.

This has been proven by neuropsychologists with actual brain scans that this is true. It is also shown with fitness. When we workout, we tear the small muscle fibers, and when we rest, we recover these fibers, and they grow. In the opposing side of this, as we stop exercising and do not push the fibers to fatigue and grow during recovery instead, they shrink and is why in turn muscle is burned as energy or stored and transformed into fat, and you become smaller or bigger. When things begin to become harder after you start, this shift is right.

That means you have stepped up and are now being tested by the universe on how well you're solution mentality has developed. So work on yourself. That is the first real step every day. Start to really make sense of what is noise and what is an acceptable volume of balance for you. It will take trial and error, but the more in tune you are with yourself and the more clarity you have, then the sooner and the more abrupt the shift will be when it happens. Then you can work on the other step to this.

So in conclusion of this book all I wish is that you now have an understanding as to how to become fulfilled in life, and also hope that you took some sort of insight enough to be able to refer back to certain things and work on others that you feel may be lacking in your life. It's never too late to change, and it's never too early to change. Change all of that energy and transfer it into positive and productive ideas to begin executing on. This is your adventure nobody else's and doesn't ever let anyone tell you differently either. Not even that voice of doubt in the back of your mind. Learn to quiet the ego and only listen to the humbled spirit. Don't fall into the traps of negative thought and emotion. Learn to control every part of your life and become better every single day.

Ultimately that's what it is about is taking care of what you can today to help further and strengthen your beliefs that much more. Too many people feel neglected, too many people feel insecure, too many people feel like they do not belong, and too many people feel as though they will never be worthy of greatness. It may not be fancy cars and clothes, but at the same rate, that is only an influence provided by the big companies that are needing you to spend money. We idolize and emulate the things that hinder us as opposed to growth with us, and it's because nobody likes to be uncomfortable. Discomfort causes change, and that change is powered by aggressive action. That's what it will take to shift the narrative for you as it did me.

It took a long time to realize how safe I was, and how it led to becoming less secure because of the lack of preparation at that point. When we become comfortable and relaxed we notice less, we become less aware, we are not fully able to catch the things that have begun decontaminated our minds and our thought patterns. Remember to keep guard and always to be getting better every day. Certain things become more effortless the process will become smoother and the smoother the process, the less hectic everything seems so, the more clarity you have for the vision and not the doubt and excess worry entangled in there as well.

So much has gone into writing this book and I have put everything I have been affected by. Everything you've read I've felt and been through to the furthest extent possible. Still does not compare to what others go through daily but whether you're running a business or are a middle-class worker just trying to make ends meet, I wanted to be someone that could provide hope to the ones that feel they may not have it. I want people to feel fulfilled and be happy in life. I want to inspire people to go for what they love, not some celebrity that has influenced the wrong material things like success and not shown the true meaning of it all.

Most people don't see the behind the scenes, and so the result is what they aim to become, but it's the behind the scenes avenue that should be referred to in the pursuit for guidance in a particular area. My goal was to change my narrative. Upon doing so, now it is to help to improve yours as well. To make you feel like you can become more than you are because you have limitless potential and you have time to correct any mistakes you have made. I hope if you're really doing this, you begin to take every second into account and cherish it because those breaths you are taking right now are all you have.

Start to make the shift and notice what is going well in your life. Do more of that and less of the things that are hindering your success. I just want to put here also that none of this is easy and all of it took me 26 years to realize. The power of progression and the growth I've experienced is what keeps me going, and my goal in life is to make sure that it can and will do the same for you as well. So I will leave you with this quote that sums up the basis for what this book is ultimately attempting to portray, and that is;

"Ideas are shit. Execution is the game" - Gary Vaynerchuk

Stage Six: The Final Footsteps

Upon the departure, to the last leg of the race, he was feeling more confident than ever. He was grateful for this entire opportunity, and he had absolutely all of the momentum in the world now, almost as if he was a tiny snowball that morphed into a mighty avalanche down a treacherous mountain. Now he was moving with more strut in his step much as the first part of the race when he had just begun. He had also met people he would have never gotten the chance to meet otherwise. He felt privileged to have been able to take this journey. He still handles all of the pain, but he feels the abundance of life much more.

With the inner journey he had undergone, he felt a new sense of fulfillment as well. He went from wanting to win to now wanting everyone else to win. He was eager to get home because he felt like he was a new person. Like the possibilities were endless now for what he could accomplish. In addition to that, he was utterly humbled by the amount of accomplishment he'd already had so far. He reflected for a moment on the nights where his family would eat together, and he felt in his heart the reason why he was always running. To specifically run away. Runaway to better days but those nights are the real wins. He forgot that. He was so anxious to alter his life. He never realized how beautiful it actually was. The desert and this marathon had changed all of that.

He began out of fear. Fear in the dream as well as anxiety on the flight over. Fear of his own potential. Mixed with so many forms of Inflictions on himself along with comparing himself to others as he watched countless strides run passed him. Different kinds of distractions, such as not having water or the blisters that were finally healing. He overcame his ego, he couldn't just give excuses anymore, he needed to keep moving and that in turn made all of what was happening real at those moments. He accepted the fact that he couldn't change what happened, nor the outcome, but he can be present and be at his best now. He thwarted his false expectations and really came into himself and also became aware of who he is because he asked all of those more profound questions that are never usually cared about. The race, for many of us, is something we're wanting to finish and rush through. If

Jericho hadn't gone through his journey, however, he would have only still been pounding more nails as a hammer looking for accomplishment after accomplishment. There's a reason people keep coming back even though it's the driest place on earth. It's because it nourishes their souls. Grounds them, and now it has grounded him in ways he would have never thought possible.

Jericho finally discovered and ignited a newly formed passion of not winning but by taking another step. He finally came to grips with the burning desire inside of him always hungry for more and transmuted that into his own self-worth, gaining a new level of humility now to take on more than he ever thought he could. Openly growing throughout the entire process. He finishes the race in San Pedro De Atacama where there are tons of people all waiting to cheer everyone on. He looks up one last time and closes his eyes as he crosses the finish line. He receives a medal and some incredible acknowledgment, unconditional love, and real, present feelings of fulfillment and joy. He is now ready to rest and go home to tell all of his family and friends everything he had learned along the way. His journey is not over. He still wants to take on the other races as well, but for right this moment he is done. He can be present and whole. He will always run, only now he is running with purpose. Not to run to or from anything, but to simply run because it cycles through every emotion he has ever felt. It brings him clarity from within himself. So he runs, he rests, runs, rests. He is fully there fully aware, and just like life, the cycle continues. He knows now that whatever he decides, he is the path.

Bibliography

Books:

Lee, Stanley. "*Venom: Lethal Protector Part One of Six.*" Venom, Vol #1, Issue #1, Marvel Comics. 1993.

Travis B. *Emotional Intelligence 2.0. TalentSmart. 2009. Print.*

Paulo C. *The Alchemist. HarterTorch. 1993. Print.*

Bronnie W. *The Top Five Regrets of Dying: A Life Transformed by the Dearly Departed. Hay House, Inc. 2012. Print.*

Movies:

Marv Films/Lionsgate/Plan B Entertainment, *Kick-Ass (2010)*

Marvel Studio's, *Thor: Ragnarok (2017)*

Online:

YouTube Video, "*Will Smith Bungee Jumps Out of a Helicopter!" 2018.*

You Tube Video Tedx Talk With Alison Ledgerwood, "*Getting Stuck in the Negatives (and How to Get Unstuck).*" *2013.*

YouTube Video Tedx Talk with Carol S. Dweck, *"The Power of Believing That You Can Improve." (2014)*

Anthony, J. R. *Do You Need to Feel Significant.* Tonyrobbins.com. (Online)

Lea, L. W. *(2005) the Mind's Mirror,* American Psychology Association (Online), Vol 36, #9

Alzheimer Disease International *(2015). Dementia Statistics*. www.alz.co.uk. (Online).

Racing the Planet – *(2019) Atacama Ultra Marathon.* Racingtheplant.com. (Online)

Marilynn, M.D, MD JD *(2017) There Are 27 Different Emotions,* Psychology Today. (Online)

Giacomo R. *(2011) Reflecting on Behavior: Gives a Tour of the Mirror Mechanism.* Association for Psychological Science. (Online).

Christine, C.C *(2017), the Secret to Controlling Your Emotions - Before They Control You,* Forbes (Online)

David, H. M.D., P.H.D. *(2017) Power vs. Force.* Forbes (Online).

Chapman University. *(2017) Survey of American Fears.* Blogs.chapman.edu. (Online)

Acknowledgements

I would like to thank my wife, Kaitlyn. Without her and her tremendous patience, I never would have been able to find myself nor this calling that has set forth a new opened door that I get to explore now as her husband. My amazing kids Jeremy and Raelynn, as well as my dog Mia. They have always been my support system and have always been there to fully accept me and keep me feeling alive! They are the best kids a father could ask for!

I would also like to thank my entire family. My mom, Evelyn, for being there and working to make sure we had everything we needed. My dad Samuel Martinez III, for ultimately being one of my best friends in addition to Coach from kindergarten all the way to 17 years old. As well as my sisters Gabriella and Ashley, and my brother Estevan for always being there for me and always staying connected and close even though life has a way of distracting us in different ways.

I would also like to give my brother-in-law, Raymond, an enormous acknowledgment for allowing me to take care of my family and also always challenging me in just the right ways.

Lastly, I would like to thank all of the people that have not only supported this book, but also have supported the journey I've been on as well. This includes amazing individuals such as; Hunter Melson, Ron Carter, Tony Vic, Kiefer Hogge, Jason Rigby, Giovanni Scott, Carlos Malave, Alex Galaviz, James Watkins, Johnny Martinez, Ian Santos, Jonathan Sawyer, Devon Boyce and Dave Skiman.

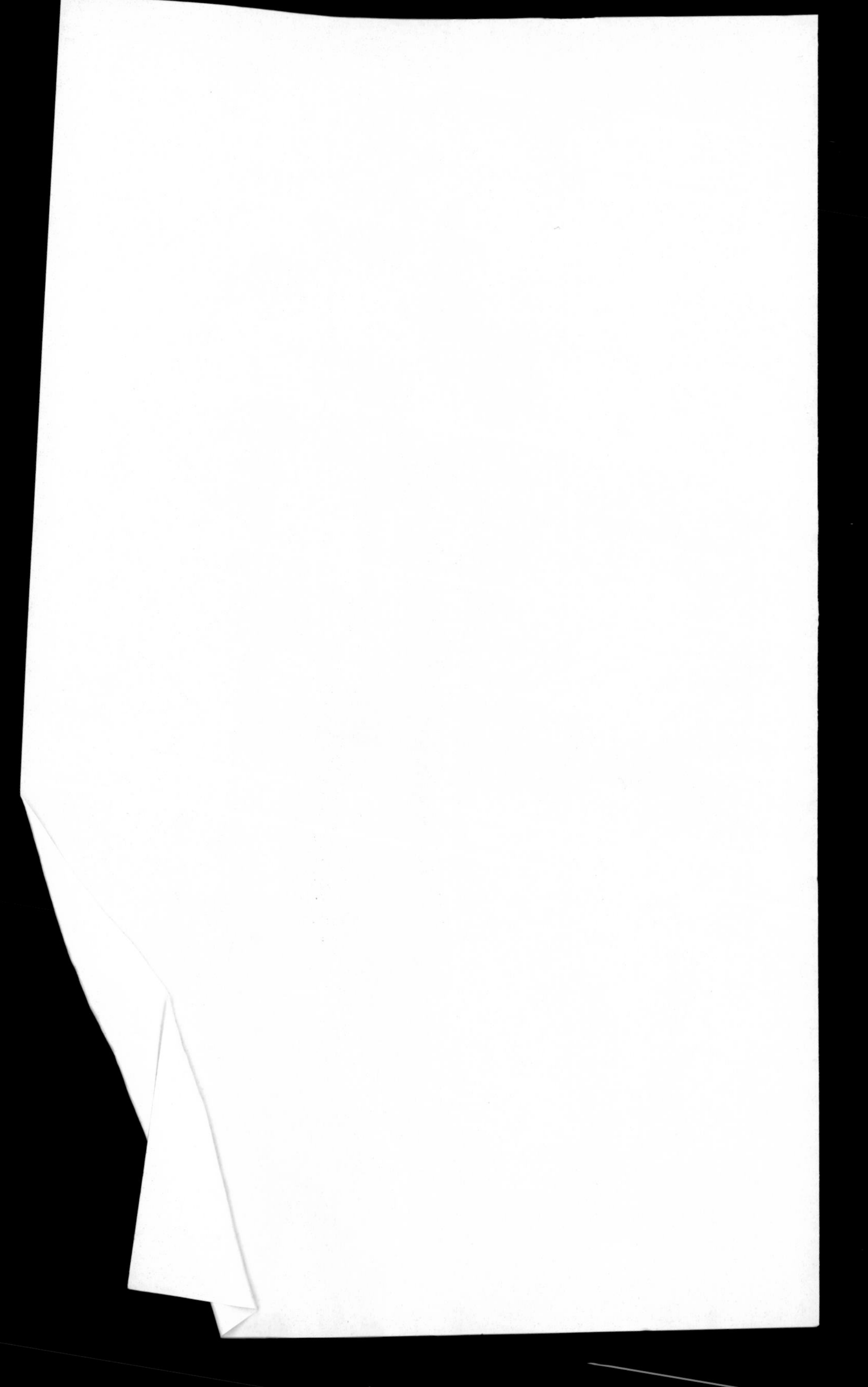

Made in the USA
Las Vegas, NV
24 December 2021

39320602R10121